A **FLESH** & **BLO**

C000233659

POWER

A FAMILY MEMOIR

WITH DERMOT KEYES

HEROBOOKS

HEROBOOKS

PUBLISHED BY HERO BOOKS
1 WOODVILLE GREEN
CO. DUBLIN
IRELAND

Hero Books is an imprint of Umbrella Publishing

First Published 2023

Copyright © Richie Power Snr and Richie Power Jnr,
& Dermot Keyes

Without limiting the rights under copyright reserved above, no part of this publication
may be reproduced, stored in or introduced into a retrieval system, or transmitted in any
form or by any means (electronic, mechanical, photocopying, recording or otherwise)
without the prior written permission of the publisher of this book.

A CIP record for this book is available from the British Library

ISBN 9781910827727

Cover design and formatting: jessica@viitaladesign.com
Photographs: Sportsfile, and the Power family collection

DEDICATION

To Ann Power (née Duggan)
A devoted wife and wonderful mother.
Thank you for everything.

And to Jamie, Stephanie, Celine Mary RIP,
John and Suzanne: memories and gratitude.

CONTENTS

ACKNOWLEDGEMENTS

★★★

RICHIE SNR

BOTH RICHIE AND myself have really enjoyed looking back on our respective hurling careers over the past few months. It's triggered a lot of memories and conversations amongst the family that we'd probably never have had only for it!

Everything that we've ever done as a family was made possible thanks to an abundance of kindness and teamwork. No-one could have asked for a greater team mate in life than I've had in Ann.

From loading the Barry's Tea van for work the following morning while I was gone training, to raising our children with great care and a sense of fun, I know how fortunate a husband I am. Ann is the cornerstone that has made a million things happen for the children and myself.

Sharing this story with Richie has been a great pleasure, a welcome reminder of all the evenings the whole lot of them were out the front of the house, pucking the sliotar over and back, dreaming of glory days in Croke Park.

To think that Jamie, John and Richie all got to share in the joy of winning an All-Ireland club title in Croke Park with Carrickshock – with Ann, Stephanie, Suzanne and myself watching on – is the stuff dreams are made of.

The only way that day could have been bettered was if Celine Mary, whom we sadly lost at the outset of life, was there celebrating with us. She's with us every day. Ann and I are proud of them all. Being grandparents to Ruairí, Leah, Richie Óg, Anna and Doireann means we get to have all the fun, while relinquishing responsibility! There's no lovelier sound in the world than a child's laughter.

Thanks to my brothers, Maurice, Pat, William and John, and to all my hurling colleagues that I soldiered with, playing with Carrickshock – and to the wonderful officers who have faithfully run our great club, all of whom couldn't have been more helpful.

To all my teammates whom I proudly wore the black and amber jersey with over the years, to the managers and selectors, to the county board officers, and the great Kilkenny supporters, thank you all.

To the friendships Ann and I forged in Cork, the late Tom Whelan, his wife Tess, and my great Kilkenny comrade, Frank Cummins, thanks for everything.

And a big thank you both to Liam Hayes of Hero Books for suggesting this project to Richie and myself, and to Dermot Keyes, who helped to assemble all of the constituent parts into a beginning, middle and end.

I hope you will enjoy the read.

Richie Power Snr
September 2023

★★★

RICHIE JNR

MANY, MANY THANKS to my parents, Richie and Ann, for their love and support over the years, especially my dad who was the biggest influence on my career. Without his presence, and guidance, I'm not so sure I would have been able to build the hurling career I have so enjoyed.

A huge thank you also to my partner, Maria, for all she has done for me over the past three years and for her continued support during my managerial career, both to date and looking towards future challenges. To my boys, Ruairí and Richie Óg, I've nothing but gratitude for all the colour and fun you have added to my life.

My brothers, Jamie and John, and sisters, Stephanie and Suzanne, have been rocks of support throughout my life and I'm forever thankful for all the times they've been there for me.

It's only right that I acknowledge my schools, Stoneyford NS and St Kieran's College, for everything they did for me during my formative years and for helping to mould me both as a hurler and a person. In primary school, Tom Duggan coached me for three years and was a massive help in guiding me through my formative years. Special thanks to all the coaches and managers who helped me from day one and guided me into inter-county hurling and for all their help, both on and off the field, when times were tough.

A massive thanks to Carrickshock, the club to whom I owe everything, and without whom I would never have had the opportunity to fulfil my dream of wearing the black and amber jersey – and for giving me the special memory of captaining Kilkenny to a minor All-Ireland and climbing the steps of the Hogan Stand eight times as a senior player. Míle buíochas.

To all the players I shared a dressing room with, both in Carrickshock and Kilkenny, thanks for being a part of my journey. To all the opposing players I shared the pitch with, thank you for pushing me to become a better player.

Finally, a huge thanks to Liam Hayes and the Hero Books team for giving dad and myself the opportunity to bring this book to life. It's something that we will treasure forever. And to Dermot Keyes, for the many, many hours he gave sitting with us all, and for building the book you now have in your hands.

Hopefully, in years to come, my kids and grandkids will leaf through it and relive many of the great days that we enjoyed with club and county.

Richie Power Jnr
September 2023

SAT IN THE Hogan Stand press box at the 1999 All-Ireland hurling final, the same date – September 12 – upon which I'm writing this acknowledgment 24 years later, I could have only dreamt of writing a book which touches on the greatest day in Irish sport. Yet here I am, thrilled and honoured to have helped share the story of two Kilkenny hurling greats, father and son, both named Richie Power. Outstanding stickmen who graced the Croke Park stage in the famed black and amber time and time again. An incredible 11 Celtic Crosses between them.

Of course, they're not the only All-Ireland senior champions in their household; John won a brace in 2014 and '15, famously finding the net, just as Richie Jnr did, in the 2014 replay win over Tipperary. Just as their father did in the 1983 senior final win over Cork. What a fabulous slice of history to share.

To Richie Snr and Richie Jnr, thanks so much for sitting with me over multiple interviews, over multiple cups of tea and something sweet in Stoneyford. A project like this isn't possible without hard work – but it was well and truly worth it.

To Ann, Jamie, John, Stephanie and Suzanne, thanks so much for taking the time to sit with me and chat about the highs, lows and all the in-betweens. This is as much a family story as it's a hurling memoir and it wouldn't have been possible without your enthusiasm and respective insights.

To John Knox, Enda McEvoy, Nicky Brennan, Tom Hogan and Adrian Finan, heartfelt thanks for making time for me during the assembly of this book and for steering me in the right direction. All have done Kilkenny hurling outstanding service through their various, highly decorated roles, so to piggy-back upon their wisdom proved invaluable.

Thanks so much to Liam Hayes for entrusting me with this account. It's the second book we've collaborated on over the past two years and I was honoured to convert this idea into the latest addition to Kilkenny's hurling library.

Finally, to my partner Avril for her support and patience; my book-loving daughter, Bronwyn; my mother, Therese; my siblings, Gavin, Kathy, John, Kevin and Lillian, and their families; and those fondly remembered – my father, Johnny, brother, Shane and my wonderful Keyes (Kit and Jimmy) and O'Hara (Lily and Terry) grandparents – they'll be forever and fondly remembered.

Hurling is a miraculous sport. And it remains one of the privileges of my life to be associated with it.

Dermot Keyes
September 2023

INTRODUCTION

'All art contains an element of pain and requires a taste for effort.'

- Arsène Wenger

THE HOME OF Ann and Richie Power is not bedecked by the many garlands and trinkets that this hurling-obsessed family has earned over six honour-laden decades.

Yes, there are a few photographic memories of glory days in Croke Park dotted around the house, while there's a kitchen press wedged full of match programmes and newspaper cuttings, but there's not a hint of ostentation at play.

Hurling is never far from the tip of any tongue once you cross the Power threshold, nor is a pot of tea, along with something sweet to accompany it… and repeat servings of good humour.

From the day Richie Jnr welcomed me in for this book's first interview on February 15, 2023, this was a household which exuded warmth – and humility.

Remarkably, even by Kilkenny standards, there are 13 Celtic Crosses under this roof, at the tail end of the village of Stoneyford, won by three proud Carrickshock men, all of whom have scored All-Ireland senior final goals. Richie Senior netted against Cork in 1983 as the black and amber completed a 'double double' of league and championship titles, a rare feat in that era for any county. Richie Junior and his brother John both goaled in the 2014 final replay victory over Tipperary, the penultimate MacCarthy Cup success of the Brian Cody era – Richie's seventh and John's first prized medal.

Some of the many medals the Powers have won for both club and county may end up on a plaque or inside a frame yet in the homestead, but there's clearly no rush on that front either.

Both men's commitment to Carrickshock clearly underlines the adage about where one's GAA service begins and, more often than not, ends. Both were the outstanding players on their respective club teams and won respect the country over for their feats with Kilkenny. But in a hurling sense, nothing will ever matter more to them than their club, which represents one of the most distinctively shaped parishes on the entire island.

The eighth senior championship with Carrickshock remains elusive; a wait as long as Mayo's for Sam Maguire, extending all the way back to 1951. That neither Richie added that medal to their extensive collection still sticks in the craw. When they told me they'd swap their All-Ireland medals for one such title with the club, I required precious little convincing. They talk as straight as they shot on the many fields they graced.

Yet there's unbridled solace to be gleaned from winning an All-Ireland Intermediate Club title in 2017, when Richie Jnr, John and Jamie helped their club secure its most significant honour in just over 75 years. Surrounded by family and friends, the Powers sampled further Croke Park glory, providing Richie Jnr – he of no cartilage in his left knee – with a fairytale finish to one of the most successful careers in the history of the game.

As we sat to compile this book, Richie was in his fourth year managing Carrickshock, giving something back to the club he owes everything to from a hurling perspective. The student is now the mentor.

Meanwhile, Richie Snr, whose commitment to the club remained rock solid while working in Cork in the early to mid-1980s, is as enthused as always by both the club and the game, so much so that he took on a selector's role with the minor team at the start of 2023.

'It isn't life and death, despite what the most ardent hurling supporter might otherwise suggest,' he said. 'Living your life well and being good to yourself and those around you: now that's worth more than any medal.'

Having admitted to a gambling problem which predated the premature conclusion of his inter-county career, Richie Jnr has faced two significant personal obstacles and made the greatest investment anyone can make… in himself. That's made him a better father, partner, son and sibling. And just like his dad, Richie's love for his club, county and his sport has remained a constant.

'We just loved it all,' he admits. 'Every bit of it. There's nothing like hurling for the club. And I wouldn't swap it for anything. Personal awards never bothered me. For me it was all about the team, be it Carrickshock or Kilkenny and what I could do to help my team – and that's what I prided myself on.'

Roughly a decade ago, an old schoolmate of mine, as obsessive a Kilkenny hurling man as any I have ever met, handed me a book which I have frequently turned to over the past decade. Devoted to John Wooden (1910-2010) the legendary UCLA basketball coach, the book contains his wisdom on sport and life, explaining how and why both intertwine.

And these are words that I have frequently turned to.

'Be more concerned with your character than your reputation.
Character is what you really are. Reputation is what people say you are.
Reputation is often based in character – but not always.
Character is how you react to things – sensibly, without getting carried away
by yourself or your circumstances.'

The character of the Power family, champions many times over, has never, ever been in doubt. To help both men share their story has been a singular privilege.

Dermot Keyes
July 23, 2023
(All-Ireland Senior Hurling Final Day)

PROLOGUE

★★★

RICHIE SNR

OLLIE WALSH WAS something else.

The first night we were in training for the 1991 All-Ireland final, I was the first player out and Ollie was standing in the middle of the field.

'Ollie,' I said, 'We're good enough to win this All-Ireland.'

My father and mother would have been in Carrick-on-Suir a lot given that our home place in Hugginstown is only a few hills away from Carrick, so I was really looking forward to playing against Tipp in an All-Ireland final. It's the one I'd really love to have won, growing up only a few miles from the county boundary.

And I was gutted when we lost; it was a far worse feeling than when we'd lost to Galway in '87. I was in absolute bits coming home that night. We could have got over the line but when you're wearing a county jersey, you're going to have a few days like that when things don't go your way.

1991 was Ollie's first year as Kilkenny manager and I remember him coming into the local in Stoneyford after he'd played a round of golf in Mount Juliet on St Stephen's Day that same year. I was inside having a pint when Ollie came in. He sat down alongside me.

'Do you know what, Richie,' he told me. 'I never forgot what you said to me in Nowlan Park about us being good enough to beat Tipp. I was really building for '92 and '93 but I really appreciated you saying that.'

Kilkenny went on to win the next two MacCarthy Cups, our first two in-a-row in a decade. That he called into me that day, to say that to me… it meant a lot. Ollie was a great manager and an even better man.

And whenever I think of matches with Tipp, Ollie is often in my thoughts.

Twenty-three years later, to be stood in Croke Park at the full-time whistle after Kilkenny had got the better of Tipp in the All-Ireland final replay was just brilliant. To have two sons – Richie and John – out on the field in the black and amber that day, having both scored goals… my God, what a feeling.

Now I'd be quiet enough at matches. I wouldn't be one of these wild lads, hoppin' and leppin' around the place, losing the run of myself. If I was any way like that, I'd probably stay at home – well, I'd like to think I'd be smart enough to make that decision without any encouragement from anyone else.

So, thank God I was able to sit back and enjoy the fact that all three lads hurled at different stages with the county and all won All-Ireland medals. If a fella can be thrilled, and cool and calm all at the same time, I was that day.

The fact that Richie and John both scored goals against Tipp, something I'd been lucky enough to do myself in the 1983 final, that just made the whole occasion extra special. Myself and Ann were on Cloud Nine that evening; we were just so thrilled for them both to be playing, so for them both to end up scoring goals that day… it really felt like a once in a lifetime day for us as a family.

It might have been Richie's seventh All-Ireland medal, but it was John's first – and after the year Richie had just put behind him, it felt like his first too. They got a hold of each other directly after the full-time whistle, which was a great moment for both of them. They made a bit of history that day, over 30 years after I'd scored a goal and won my first Celtic Cross with Kilkenny.

Fast forward a year and Kilkenny have retained the MacCarthy Cup after beating Galway. Following the presentation, Richie got those few minutes out on the field, pucking the ball with Ruairí and there were a few smashing photos taken. John Knox, who covered all the great days the county had with the *Kilkenny People* for over 40 years, managed to get out onto the field to grab a few quick words with a few of the lads, including Richie, whom he made a beeline for.

'Richie replied, as mannerly as always… John, would you mind if I just have a few moments with Ruairí, just to savour this… and we can have the chat afterwards?' And he was true to that. He was in the moment, he wanted to live in that moment and treasure it with the young lad and it was very personal to him.

'It was a great moment for the two of them and then he did have the chat with me afterwards. He was in charge of everything there and then. Now he may not have been fully prepared for what followed a few months later but, at the same time, he was the one with the aching knee. He probably knew that there's little or nothing left in the knee in terms of hurling so he took his moment.

'And I'm sure every time he's been to Croker since then, he's had a look down at that spot on the field and thought of 2015… and that puckabout with his son.'

During Brian Cody's time in charge, along with Richie and John, the Carrickshock club had Michael Rice, John Tennyson and John Dalton all heavily involved in successful All-Ireland days with the county. We might never have an era like that in the parish again.

Sure, you couldn't be anything other than proud of that level of achievement. It was a tremendous time in all of our lives and I'll be forever grateful for it.

★★★

RICHIE JNR

WE BEAT TIPPERARY in the 2014 All-Ireland final replay by three points (2-17 to 2-14) and both myself and my brother John found the net. I really felt we deserved it; in fact, we should have won by more. When the final whistle went, I collapsed to my knees and a year's load of emotion just started flowing out of me.

I was crying on the ground, and all that was going through my mind was where I'd been the previous autumn to where I was at that moment, having won my seventh All-Ireland senior medal.

John was the first player over to me – sure you couldn't script it – it's even hard to describe the surge of emotion that was running through me during those moments. Any of the lads that came over to celebrate with me could see the tears in my eyes and a few of them must have been thinking *What the f**k is wrong with this lad?* I'd never reacted to any of our previous All-Ireland wins like this one.

Don't get me wrong, the euphoria in 2011 and '12 was incredible and I was just mad to embrace everyone and make the most of those great days too.

But this one felt different. It really did, given all that had gone on in the previous year, mentally dealing with my knee problem as best I could, and then building myself up to play in the final. Add into that admitting to my problem with gambling, piecing things back together off the field and then doing all I could to put things right from both a personal and hurling perspective. I'd a lot going on, let's face it.

Lots of plates that I needed to keep spinning.

So, to fall on my knees in tears when we'd won? It just a huge relief.

Scoring three goals over the two finals and John getting a goal too… meaning the two of us and dad had all scored goals in All-Ireland finals. It's hard to take that in now, eight years later… that we've all done that. I'd proven to myself that I could get back to that level. All the hard work had been worth it.

I'd had days in the Hotel Kilkenny car park when I just wanted to pack it in. But the one-on-one training with Mickey Comerford kept me going, kept driving me on – and I kept training with him even after I'd rejoined the panel.

Enda McEvoy, who has written many a kind word about Kilkenny and myself over the years, generously described my contribution to the drawn final in the *Irish Examiner* as follows:

'If one man has been the championship-breaker for Kilkenny these past two months, it's been Richie Power. Introduced a minute after Shefflin at the three-quarter stage against Limerick, it was he rather than his more celebrated fellow redhead who turned the issue Kilkenny's way. He was rightly praised for his second goal three weeks ago but wasn't given his due for his technically astonishing first goal: a feather-light touch to dink the sliotar over (Darren) Gleeson and meet it on the other side. Kilkenny would not have won had not Power, the county's most naturally gifted player since DJ Carey, come into his kingdom at the right moment.'

The following year, we won another All-Ireland after beating Galway (1-22 to 1-18). It was my eighth senior winners' medal. I'd got back into the match day panel and onto the field for the concluding 12 minutes, and I was delighted to be involved after another tough year, having torn a posterior cruciate ligament against Galway in Tullamore 14 months previously.

In the 10 months that followed that injury, I had three operations.

One way or the other, those three operations helped me get 12 more minutes in another All-Ireland final.

Twelve minutes more than most hurlers have ever experienced.

With the cup back in our dressing-room, Croke Park virtually empty and strips of gold tinsel on the field, I'd a puck around with Ruairí. And given what only lay around the corner for me at that time, that puck around has taken on another level of significance for me. There I was, with my son, not knowing then that this would be the last time I'd ever wear the Kilkenny jersey.

One of the lads' hurls was on the ground and I told Ruairí to pick it up, and we pucked the ball for about five minutes. There were a few lovely photos taken from pitch level and the press box, and I'm so glad of them now – I might well have been the first Kilkenny player to have a child out on the field after an All-Ireland back in 2011 and I brought him around the field with me. Ruairí won't remember the first few years, but he'll remember 2015 and I hope that'll always be special for him.

It's incredibly special to me and I'd imagine it'll feel all the more special the older I get. Sure, it was probably the perfect ending, really.

Even when we got back into the dressing-room, the whole thing felt surreal, thinking back to that meeting I'd had with the management in Hotel Kilkenny in October, 2013, when I genuinely didn't know if I'd be back in a county jersey again.

I went home that evening and said to myself, *Your inter-county career is finished.*

It's over.

It's done.

You had a good run but that's the end of it.

Full stop.

So, to get back into that jersey again and to win two more All-Irelands was massive. I'd proven something to myself and, in the back of my mind at the very least, to Brian Cody and Mick Dempsey as well. Sometimes I would have felt like telling them that they were wrong to do what they did, but maybe they were right to do what they did in order to get the reaction that they got out of me.

Some people might think differently about all of that, but I don't really think about it too much now. But when the final whistle went in 2014, it was the most surreal moment I'd ever had as a hurler.

Look what you've done. You've come from rock bottom.

The lowest ebb of your life.

And here you are, with another All-Ireland won.

And by Jesus, Power, did you play your part in this one. No-one can ever deny that. No-one can ever take this feeling away from you – and the whole hurling world watching you.

You've earned this.

Your first All-Ireland winning season that you weren't gambling through.

You've really f***ing earned this.

There was more than a hint of Rocky about it all, in hindsight.

'He's been knocked out, just when he ought to be in his prime. Will he be able to get back to the top? Will he wear the belt again?'

I did… and even allowing for having to retire from inter-county hurling at 29, life's been pretty good ever since then.

A FATHER'S DEVOTION TO FAMILY, CLUB AND COUNTY

Richie Power Snr is introduced to the crowd as the Kilkenny All-Ireland winning 1982 and '83 teams are honoured at Croke Park before the 2007 All-Ireland final between Kilkenny and Limerick.

Richie Snr's parents, Statia and Ned and (below) Richie Snr and Jnr in the company of the Liam MacCarthy Cup in 2008 and also Richie Snr's brothers, Maurice, William, Pat and John.

Stephanie (7), Richie (3) and Jamie (8) after loading their dad's Barry's Tea van, and (below) celebrating Richie Jnr's Communion in 1993 (from left, Jamie, Richie Snr, Baby John, Ann, Richie Jnr and Stephanie).

The Carrickshock team which won the Kilkenny Junior Hurling Championship in 1979, with five Power brothers all on board.

Richie Snr and John accepting the trophy after Kilkenny won the 1998 All-Ireland Masters Championship in Croke Park, when both Richie Snr and Jamie hurled on Leinster final day, and (below) the family relax back at home that evening (from left) Jamie, Suzanne, Richie Jnr, John and Richie Snr).

After celebrating Jamie and Noelle's wedding in 2019 (from left, John, Suzanne, Jamie, Ruairi, Richie and Stephanie) and (below) three generations of Powers... Richie Jnr, Ruairi, Richie Snr, Jamie and John.

All the family in 2019 (Stephanie, Richie Snr, Ann, John, Ruairi, Richie Jnr, Suzanne and Jamie) and (below) Richie Snr and Ann on holiday in 2018 on Sunset Beach.

Richie Snr evades the clutches of Galway's Conor Hayes during the 1982 All-Ireland semi-final and (right) and he is chaired off the field by friends Noel Maher and PJ Ronan (RIP) after Kilkenny's defeat of Cork in the final.

Richie was the sole Kilkenny award winner when the 1986 All Star team was announced and (below) flanked by his great friend, Frank Cummins and his brother, Joe.

The Kilkenny team which defeated Cork in the 1982 All-Ireland final

The Kilkenny 1982 and 1983 All-Ireland winning Jubilee teams are honoured in Croke Park, 25 years after their dual triumph

Richie and his management team which led Kilkenny to the 1999 All-Ireland under-21 title (from left) John Marnell (Dicksboro), Murty Kennedy (St Lachtain's), Richie Snr and Eamonn Hennessy. And Richie on managerial duty with Carrickshock minors in 2001 (below) and also leading Castletown during the Laois Senior Championship two years later.

I

Carrickshock:
Alpha and Omega

★★★

★★★

JOHN KNOX

(*Kilkenny People* Chief GAA Reporter and Sports Editor: 1974-2010)

CARRICKSHOCK IS A small club which played a huge role in Kilkenny's success under Brian Cody – but you can't consider Carrickshock without thinking about the Powers. The club's prominence has been Power-induced. The Powers are the club and the club are the Powers – not exclusively, of course – but you can't underestimate their contribution either. If you get a family that buys in fully, like the Fennellys did with the Shamrocks, then the Powers are their equivalent in the neighbouring parish. Richie Snr was chairman of the club while he was playing inter-county, and then you've Ann, who is another staunch club member.

When Richie Snr was playing, and working for Barry's Tea, often there'd be loads delivered to the house and Ann would unload it while Richie was at training. The family never made a distinction between club and family. Club was family... and family was club. They're great people and so down to earth. And if you fell out with the Powers, there must be something wrong with you. You just couldn't.

They're just that type of people. To me, they epitomise what a GAA family is all about. It's about giving. It's about the volunteers. It's about parking your ego and always parking it. They're just great people – and the whole club is like that.

There are certain parts of every county where this applies but you'd have parts of Kilkenny where people would be edgy, but I never found that edginess in Carrickshock. There's always been a warmth and a welcoming feel to the parish. Now that doesn't mean they wouldn't tell you that you played a poor ball during a match or so on but that'd be it, they'd say it to you but it'd be said without any malice and then it's parked.

There's a nice atmosphere about that club and they proudly carry their history well – and it's a rich history.

★★★

RICHIE SNR

CONDONSTOWN, IN THE South Kilkenny townsland of Hugginstown, is my home place, while Stoneyford, where we raised the five lads and still live today is at the opposite end of the peculiarly shaped parish of Hugginstown, Newmarket and Stoneyford.

This is a physically divided parish – I actually have to leave the parish to get to Carrickshock's field in Hugginstown, which is a 15-minute drive from Stoneyford. I either go through Dunnamaggin or, if I use the main road, I actually pass through Ballyhale. Where we live is less than a mile from the parish of Ballyhale and I have to drive through two or three miles of that parish to get back into my own parish. I've asked more people in different counties if they know of any club in a similar situation to ours, and I've yet to meet someone who can confirm that there is.

Years and years ago, there was a divide in our parish, when Stoneyford and Hugginstown had separate teams, and when the parish came together they called the club Carrickshock (Carraig-Seabhac – the hawk's rock). In December 1831, there was a battle in the townland of Carrickshock which the *Irish Examiner* referenced in its 2010 Kilkenny senior hurling final preview:

'An armed police column, which was protecting the 'Proctor', Edmond Butler, as he collected a tithe to support the local Protestant clergy – a tithe to which the locals vehemently objected – clashed with a large crowd, which resulted in the deaths of 17 people, 13 of whom were members of the constabulary. Let's listen to the poet, Richard Lahert...

Then lithe as mountain hare,
And that is not a vaunt –
James Treacy grabbed the proctor,
Saying: 'This is the man we want!'
A peeler grabbed the proctor back,
'Twas but a brief respite,
For Butler's skull was broken
By rock and mallet smite.
Pitchfork, scythe and hurley
Were used to maim and kill
In that brief but savage battle
That makes one shudder still.

The monument where the battle occurred remains our club crest to this day. As a club, we had a core of brilliant people who kept the whole thing going; people like Sean Raggett, who was a great man to have at the top table for so many years in a variety of roles, be it secretary or chairman. If the likes of Sean hadn't been so strong-willed at the time, we might have ended up with two teams at either end of the parish again. It's still an issue and we've lost a few lads over the years to other clubs. But all in all, we've just got on with things as best we can and it remains a great club that I've huge affection for, and pride in, and that'll always be the case.

I was the middle child. Maurice and Pat are older than me, with William and John the younger two. Growing up, our lives were divided between farming and hurling, and nothing else got a look-in. During the long summer nights, my mother must have been fed up calling us in.

Before we'd come in, the jumpers used to be half-flung off us and we'd be coated in sweat after hurling for hours, and we'd be only fit for bed when we eventually paid heed to her. But those nights out in the field below the farm, I always felt that Maurice and Pat could have been better than me.

Maurice was very unlucky. He was a sub in 1982 and had been on the panel for a while. But after the League in '82, himself and John Lawlor, the Lord have mercy on him, were both dropped from the panel. Maurice was a great wing-forward. He had heaps of pace and skill, while Pat was as good a corner-back as you'd get… whereas I was the one who got that bit more luck along the way.

Christie Twomey was the teacher who looked after the school league team. Christie was a Cork man and I really looked up to him because of the way he trained us and looked after us so well. There was another man called Jimmy Hearne, who did an awful lot of work behind the scenes. He was the first man into the yard at home the Tuesday morning after I won a minor All-Ireland medal in 1975 to congratulate me.

We hurled in his field and the matches we played on Sundays down there, when I look back on them all, playing the likes of Lismatigue and Booleyglass, sure they were great days. Christie and Jimmy were a great influence and steered a lot us in the right direction at underage level.

Where I grew up is only a short distance from Carrick-on-Suir and my mother, Statia, would have shopped more often in Carrick than she ever did in Kilkenny city. She'd have gone down to Waterford from time to time as well.

MY HOME PLACE is closer to Waterford than the roundabout before the Springhill Court Hotel on the approach to the Kilkenny city ring road. In Kilkenny terms, we'd be considered deep south people.

Being not too far from the Waterford border, sure you'd always keep an eye on how the neighbours are doing in hurling terms, and it's a crying shame they didn't get over the line in either the 2017 or 2020 All-Ireland finals. And who knows, the ship might well have sailed for that group of players now, talented and all as so many of them are. It's not that simple to get back to All-Ireland senior finals.

You can make a good comparison between Kilkenny and Waterford in All-Ireland terms as you can with my own club, which hasn't won a senior county title since 1951 (our seventh) and us being next door to the Shamrocks with their 20 county senior titles and nine All-Irelands. There's even a couple of players living in our parish who go down and hurl with the Shamrocks, but look, that's their decision. But it is disappointing.

From around the age of 14, I would have suffered with asthma, particularly during the winter, and I used to find it difficult to see out 65 minutes on account of it. I remember my mother bringing me down to the doctor in Ballyhale – she had a path worn to the place with me, the poor woman. The doctor's message couldn't have been any clearer: 'You won't play much sport when you're older. You just can't afford to be getting wet.'

For a young lad like me who was mad into sport, that news was like getting hit over the head with a sledgehammer. I was still a thousand miles away from hurling senior for Kilkenny but to be told I wouldn't be able to play at all was a lot to take in. But my mother then brought me to a different doctor in the Infirmary in Waterford, and I ended up in there for the better part three weeks, getting a dozen or so injections.

Those few weeks turned me inside out and made a huge difference. Granted, in the last 10 minutes of nearly every match I'd ultimately play, the tank was generally always empty. Now that mightn't be the case nowadays given all the advances in sports medicine and respiratory care. I was taken off in a good few games, but I never minded that too much.

I USED TO run a good bit when I was a young fella.

I ran competitively while I was at Ballyhale Vocational School and I really got into it. I've no doubt all that running helped to build me up and got me physically prepared for the cut and thrust of inter-county hurling. But every year that passed, hurling took more and more of a grip on me; there we five of us at home and the spare time we spent with each other was dominated by hurling, like so many households in Kilkenny before and since.

But I loved running, especially over the longer cross-country distances... and there were a few race days in Thomastown and Tullamore out of it. Despite being told I mightn't get to play too much sport because of my asthma, I still loved to run, even if I was never going to be a contender to wear an Irish singlet. But my interest in competitive running veered off when I finished school. I still have a great grá for athletics. Running is a great leveller. The character of an athlete is laid bare in front of the watching world and the pressure on the big stage must be something else. Relays aside, it's all about the individual... it's a sport which requires enormous dedication, and tests every single fibre of the athlete.

A real hard slog.

IN MY TIME, Carrickshock would have had a serious squad. We lost county junior finals in 1975 and '77 before we finally won a junior final in '79, when we beat Graigue-Ballycallan by 3-11 to 2-7... I was 22 or 23 at the time, playing corner-forward and that win represented a real breakthrough for us. I scored 1-3 that day, and ended up being top scorer on the day.

The *Kilkenny People* captured the significance of the day for the club:

'No doubt this victory revived memories of Carrickshock's great victories in the past. They have a proud tradition having won seven senior titles and four junior titles. Their last victory was 25 years ago when they defeated Galmoy in the junior final and this week they celebrated the silver jubilee of that win... the green and white colours of the Carrickshock supporters were seen dancing on the terraces and in the stand when the final whistle sounded. Having tasted defeat on their last two visits to Nowlan Park, their victory was all the more appreciated by their jubilant supporters... Carrickshock was more or less a team of stars. However, they had some outstanding players in John Poole, Pat Power, Brendan Raggett, Dixie Burke, Maurice Power and Richard Power.'

The club was successful at senior level in the 30s, 40s and 50s (winning four in-a-row in the latter) and we'd love to have been as successful as the previous generations. We had a really good group of players, but we just couldn't get to senior. So, I've often looked back myself and wondered, what's the difference between the successful club only down the road... and then a less successful club like ours.

We had an excellent work ethic, and the numbers at training were always good, so everything was right. The top table was 100 percent, the players were 100 percent, but we just didn't get the results that we should have got.

Looking back at my own time, we were definitely good enough to have gone up to senior but we just couldn't get over the line. Just look at the way Glenmore drove on, coming up from junior to win two senior county titles and a club All-Ireland. Gowran beat us twice in three years, one of which went to a replay before they went on and won a couple of county finals. Dicksboro won the intermediate in 1991, beating us along the way and went on to win the senior title two years later.

The teams that were beating us went on to do well and even win senior, while we never got across the line. And we've been beaten in two county senior finals in the modern era, in 2010 and '13. In fact, we haven't won a senior title since the parish rule was introduced. We were so close but we still haven't got there in my lifetime. But you keep hoping.

You have to keep hoping.

★ ★ ★

RICHIE JNR

HURLING HAS BEEN part of my life since my primary school days in Stoneyford… well, for as long as I could bring a hurl in with me. Myself and my neighbour, Damien Raggett used to walk to school together and detour home via the pitch, so the love of hurling has been there pretty much for as far back as my memories extend to.

By the time I was in Fourth Class, Carrickshock came into the picture because up until then, Stoneyford and Newmarket had separate teams even though we were in the same parish. But I remember we actually played Newmarket in a county final one year and I was marking Brian Tennyson – John's brother – and he had a few years on me. He was a big buster of a lad, whereas I was small and afraid of my life of him.

But the following year, we came together as a schools' team and we were managed by Tom Duggan from Mullinavat, and he was absolutely brilliant. I only hurled for three years under him but he had a huge influence on my career. And there I was hurling alongside John Dalton, John Tennyson and Michael Rice, none of us knowing what we'd be part of with Kilkenny further down the road.

There was such a great buzz playing with them all; we just clicked. Mam did a huge amount of driving in those days, bringing five or six of us to Hugginstown straight from school and then she'd bring us home. We just loved it. And any day we weren't in Hugginstown, we were below in the field until it was dark… before we'd appear at the backdoor… caked in mud, to come in to do our homework. It was pure hurling all the way – sure Jamie and John were no different – we'd be hurling indoors, banging hurls off presses, and then we progressed to outdoors, breaking a window or two along the way.

Pucking balls, and dad out with us for much of it, joining in… sure, it was constant.

Dad coached me from under-14 all the way up to under-21 with the club and he even took over the senior team one year as well. Under dad, we won two under-16 'A' and two minor 'A' county titles, which was huge for a small club like Carrickshock to win at that level in Kilkenny. It was massive. And while we never got over the line at under-21 or senior, those were unbelievable days for the club.

And we just loved it.

Every bit of it.

There was nothing like it. And I wouldn't swap it for anything.

★★★

JOHN

MR ROCHE, WHO was our primary school principal, lived three doors up from us and he used to walk past our house every day. He often said there was always one of us outside, pucking the ball against the wall... be it myself, Jamie, Suzanne, Richie or Stephanie. Without fail, by the time he had the school doors locked and was walking back up the road, he'd see one of us out at home... hurling away.

★★★

RICHIE JNR

AT THE END of 2015, Carrickshock were relegated from the senior grade in Kilkenny. I might have won an eighth senior All-Ireland medal with the county that autumn, but between the state of my knee and the status of the club heading into 2016, being back in intermediate, my frame of mind wasn't great, naturally enough.

We'd played in the county senior final as recently as 2013, losing to Clara by two points (1-15 to 2-10). We'd missed out on a huge opportunity to do something the club hadn't done since 1951, so we're waiting as long as Mayo are for Sam Maguire. Maybe that's one of the reasons dad is such an admirer of Mayo football.

John Knox, who has reported on more Kilkenny senior finals than most, suggested we'd let the 2013 title behind us in his *Kilkenny People* match report the following week:

'Carrickshock will have regrets, serious regrets after a hard-fought decider that was nearly choked to death by the protagonists' caution, fear of losing and closing down of

each other. The 'Shock looked well placed when level at half-time (0–11 to 2–5) after playing against the strong wind. They battled their way into the lead, when sub Damien Walsh turned a hard-won ball by Pat Tennyson into the lead point (2–8 to 0–13) 10 minutes from the finish.

'They were on a roll. Within a minute Michael Rohan all but walked the ball into the net after a lovely move involving Brian Donovan and John Power sliced open the Clara defence. The ball was fouled; the goal disallowed. Momentum was still with the losers. Another Tennyson assist saw John Power shoot Carrickshock 2–9 to 0–13 clear with seven minutes remaining.

'Thus, the game arrived at the 54th minute. (Lester) Ryan's big moment. He asked 10-point man and regular free-taker, Keith Hogan, to step down from duty after Conor O'Shea had been fouled in front of the city end goal.'

Lester did his bit. He found the net and broke our hearts.

That was the closest I'd ever get to a senior medal with the club… 2013 is the year I'd love to scrub from the slate.

I've said this numerous times and I mean it, I'd trade my eight All-Ireland medals for one senior championship medal with the club. I've said it at medal presentations up north and down in Kerry, and people have almost choked on their drinks a few times when I've said that, wondering why I'd say something like that.

Your club is everything.

You pretty much orbit around it. That's where you've hurled since you were four years of age alongside the lads you grew up with. To win a senior medal is the pinnacle at club level and to win one in Kilkenny is just so f***ing hard. And we put ourselves in a position to win one with 10 minutes to go, and then we let it slip.

I've never actually watched the game back and I never will.

That's how hard it is. I suppose you live and you learn but that's a loss that will definitely go to the grave with me.

★★★

JAMIE

TO END UP in Croke Park in an All-Ireland final with the two lads in 2017 was unbelievable, but the 2013 senior final will always haunt all of us. That was our huge chance and the club still hasn't fully recovered from that.

But the intermediate win in 2017 was hugely important – it broke the fever from 2013, you could say. Despite the knee, Richie featured that year in the semi-final, was then fit enough to start the final and he ended up as Man of the Match. We hurled together for a long time, so to cap it all off with an All-Ireland in Croke Park was great.

In spite of that, and the eight All-Irelands with Kilkenny, he was still robbed. To be finished up at 29 was incredibly tough on him. We definitely hurled through the club's golden era. It's just a pity we didn't cap it off with a senior title. You'd swap at least one good day in Croke Park for one good day in Nowlan Park.

★★★

STEPHANIE

THE 2013 COUNTY senior final was the big 'what if' for all of us. It was like slow motion being there... sat in the stand, and you could sense it slipping away from them in the second-half. And I knew how hard it was on the three lads playing... and on dad as well. To be so close after being in control in the first-half. They all took that loss badly.

★★★

RICHIE SNR

I'D HAVE GIVEN anything to see Richie's squad win the senior championship but we probably didn't hurl well enough in the 2010 final against O'Loughlin Gaels, when we lost by 0-17 to 1-11. I was a selector that year... but we probably didn't hold well enough to win it. John Knox summed it up pretty neatly in his *Kilkenny People* match report:

'A late Carrickshock goal injected a bit of excitement into proceedings, but what would have been the Southerners' first success since 1951 never looked on.'

Our manager Brendan Fennelly, who moved on to manage Laois after the final, summed things up well following the full-time whistle.

'Experience was very important in the final as it turned out. O'Loughlin's had it and we didn't. We got off to a slow start and we were trying to recover all afternoon. For about 20 seconds at the finish, we had a chance of a draw but that was as near as we got... Carrickshock were good enough to contest a Kilkenny senior final.

'That makes them a good team, a very good team.

'They shouldn't sell themselves short because they lost to a good and experienced team like O'Loughlin's... There was massive momentum in the club and parish during the last few weeks. That shouldn't be allowed die.'

Three years later, we were back in another final, this time against Clara, but we left it behind us in the closing stages, having led by two points with seven minutes of regulation time remaining. Lester Ryan stuck a free into the net in the 54th minute to edge them ahead. And that ended up winning it for Clara. And we've not been as close again to landing the big one since then.

That was a real, real killer.

NICKY BRENNAN
(Kilkenny teammate of Richie Snr's and manager of Kilkenny, 1995-97)

THE PLAYING GENERATION more or less finished with Carrickshock now endured some pain, losing a couple of senior finals along the way, especially the 2013 final against Clara when they had one hand on the cup... and then in the last few minutes it was pulled away from them. The disappointment that day was written all over Richie Senior's face.

That will always be a big regret for them.

★★★

RICHIE JNR

IN 2014, WE got back to another senior semi-final, where we once again faced Clara, but they beat us very well that day (1-19 to 0-8) and then, in 2015, we were relegated. Barely two years previously, we'd been a puck of a ball from the senior title. It was quite the fall and very difficult to process. But we were determined to go straight back up and regain our competitive footing. We were going to train as hard as we could in early 2016 to get back up – I thought we were a good mid-table senior team, that'd we'd had a bad run of results that year… that we just couldn't turn the tide on.

By that time, I couldn't see myself playing again given the state of my knee, but then by May, I'd started to see some light at the end of the tunnel as my knee began to improve and I was brought on for Carrickshock in the league final against Tullaroan that September… during which I broke a knuckle in my left hand. So, I missed the intermediate quarter-final that year on account of the knuckle.

Come the semi-final, we faced Tullaroan again but I still wasn't starting games; I'd be on for the last 15 or 20 minutes. There was a big melee in that game; both Padraig Walsh and David Franks were sent off – now Padraig was hurling out of his skin that year, averaging about six points a game, so him seeing the line was a big blow to them.

The game was in the melting pot and I came on, as usual, with 15 or 20 minutes to go and we won by a point… so we'd bounced back to reach a county final where we played Tullogher. I came on a few minutes after half-time in what was a terrible game of hurling, that we won by 0-13 to 0-6. To come straight back up was brilliant and we then set off into unknown territory in the Leinster Club Championship.

WE BARELY GOT past Kiltale from Meath in the semi-final in Trim, by 2-12 to 2-9, during which I came on 12 minutes into the second-half. I picked up a yellow card that day with the *Meath Chronicle* match report later claiming… '*had it been football, the colour would have been black*'.

We played Celbridge in the Leinster final in Newbridge, a game that John Knox labelled *The Great Escape* in the *Kilkenny People*. And he wasn't wrong: with four minutes of normal time left, we were trailing by 1-14 to 0-11.

'*During the remaining seven minutes – normal plus the additional – Carrickshock threw everything but the kitchen sink at the opposition. They gained parity; fell behind and scored a hard to imagine 3-1 overall to get in front with 62:40 showing on the clock. The first time Carrickshock showed in front was at the final whistle!*'

To score three goals so late on and to end up winning by 3-12 to 1-16 was

FLESH & BLOOD SERIES

hard to credit; I can't remember being on a team that turned things around like that so late on. Our manager, Tommy Shefflin was naturally over the moon at the full-time whistle.

'Over the years Carrickshock have been on the other side of results like this, so maybe it is their turn. No-one can begrudge them this win. They kept going to the end. They never gave up. With 10 minutes to go, they were going for goals. They got the breaks eventually. You either have heart or you don't. Carrickshock have it in abundance. Okay, there was a bit of luck about the win, but good teams make their own luck sometimes too.'

Robert Emmetts from London were our All-Ireland semi-final opponents in Portlaoise and that was the first game I'd started since the relegation final the previous year... and I got through it fine. We were well ahead at half-time; they'd had two players sent off in the first-half and we ended up winning by 0-18 to 1-9. With one eye on the All-Ireland final, Tommy took me off 10 minutes into the second-half, by which time we already knew we'd be playing Ahascragh-Fohenagh from Galway in the final.

I COULDN'T BELIEVE I'd be togging out in Croke Park again just a few months after the prognosis I'd received. And it ended up being one of the most satisfying days I ever had there as a player... to win an All-Ireland title with the club, alongside Jamie and John, with all three of us on the scoresheet as well. We won comfortably in the end, by 2-15 to 0-6 and were in control right from the off.

Going up that day to Croke Park in the bus with the lads, and all the photos that were taken after the match with the family and what felt like the whole parish was very special. That was one of our best performances in years and to produce a display like that in Croke Park was so satisfying and we rightly celebrated for days and weeks after it.

It was a brilliant day to be a part of. We were back senior and we'd three trophies on the sideboard.

In hurling terms, I couldn't have hoped for a better pick me up.

★★★

NICKY BRENNAN

TO GET TO play in Croke Park again and win an All-Ireland club title with Carrickshock was something so many of us wanted to happen for Richie's sake, because by 2017, there was a recognition that he probably wasn't going to hurl beyond that year.

★★★

RICHIE JNR

IN THAT POST-2015 playing window with the club, preparation was everything. If wherever we were playing didn't have a gym, I knew I had to go to Hugginstown to do 40 minutes on the bike to get the blood flowing through my leg, before getting the knee strapped. That warm-up was vital for me.

The day of the All-Ireland final, we had to arrange things with a club in Dublin so that I had access to an exercise bike in the gym. I knew I had to do all that to give anything close to my best once the ball was thrown in. However, my style of play didn't change all that much. In 2016, I was used at centre-forward, before moving into full-forward the following year.

I didn't really want to play on the inside line, because there's so much twisting and turning to do in there, whereas when you're in and around the centre-forward position, you have that bit more freedom to roam and you're not twisting and turning as sharply as you do when you've 14 on your back. But once the game started, I forgot about playing effectively on one good knee; adrenaline takes over once the game is on.

Going back to 2014, I was used to having my knee heavily strapped and it used to take the physio 15-to-20 minutes every time. I needed the strap to be so solid… to be so held in place by tape… so, literally, my knee couldn't move.

Now, the days after a game, of course you'd suffer.

But to end up getting parts of 2016 and '17 back playing with the club, it was worth it. One hundred percent.

IN 2017, WE were back where we belonged in Kilkenny – at senior level – and I felt that I could keep going. I didn't play in any of the league games but I knew I'd something to contribute come the senior championship, and we ended up having a good campaign, reaching the quarter-final where we played James Stephens… who just got past us after a replay in Callan.

We were in such a good position at half-time in the replay, leading by 2-12 to 1-10 but the Village came back at us really strongly in the second-half to see their way through to a semi-final, where they ended up beating Ballyhale Shamrocks.

Walking off the field that day, something clicked in my head. I knew that was it. I told dad… 'I'm done.'

He was the first person I told.

'I can't keep putting my body and my head through any more of this.'

Now, I could have kept playing if I really wanted to, but I was starting to think with the bigger picture in mind. I knew I was mentally exhausted and that all boiled back to the beginning of 2015. Trying to put your body through stuff you shouldn't have to put your body through isn't sustainable. There were several factors I had to take into consideration.

How much more damage was I doing by playing?

How much worse was I making things for myself in the long run?

I had a son, and the rest of my life to take into account. So, from then on, I had to mentally prepare myself from being away from playing.

Only that wasn't completely the end.

IN 2022, I played for the junior 'A' team against our next-door neighbours, Dunnamaggin – in goal – in the county semi-final in Piltown. The previous year, I'd played in goal while also managing the team when we'd reached the county semi-final. We had no second goalie in the club and we really needed my brother, Jamie out the field. We were low on options at the time so in I went, and I really enjoyed it.

And, as the year went on, I found myself wondering why I didn't move back into the goal in 2016? Why didn't I suggest leaving Jamie out the field and that I'd play as goalkeeper?

I got to last year, and I'd decided that was definitely *that* in terms of playing. Andrew, our regular goalkeeper, who is now back with us, landed a bombshell when he told me that he'd be away the weekend the semi-final was fixed.

We approached a young lad on the junior panel, who'd played in goal a bit during his underage years, about playing for us… so, we were training the Tuesday night before the semi-final on the goal, and he ended up getting a knock. The following morning, he rang me and said he wouldn't be able to play… so I decided there and then, that if all comes to all, I'd line out in goal the following Sunday if that's what it came to.

We won the semi-final. Andrew came back, but then the final never actually got played for a variety of reasons. I also played a couple of games for the footballers in 2022 because they were struggling for numbers. I really enjoyed those run-outs and it was great being around the lads and back in a dressing room set-up as a player.

Now, we don't take football seriously within the club; it's a bit of craic. I just found it hard to say no. But I am now 100 percent done with playing.

But by God, it was fun while it lasted.

★★★

RICHIE SNR

I'D HAVE THE same attitude as Richie when it comes to the club coming before the county. We were wholeheartedly committed to Kilkenny whenever we pulled on the jersey, that goes without saying, but achieving success with Carrickshock was always number one for me. I'd have gladly exchanged my three All-Ireland medals for a senior title with the club.

I look back on that junior final we won in 1979 and I can remember coming back to the field in Hugginstown that night and it was massive for us; the club hadn't won anything for years after losing finals in 1975 and '77.

There's one thing I can state with confidence that successive Kilkenny teams have had and I can't necessarily say the same when it comes to, say, Waterford, or indeed Wexford for that matter. If you're good enough to be brought into the Kilkenny panel, it doesn't matter what club you come from. The club stuff gets parked outside the dressing-room door in Nowlan Park.

And once you're inside that door, you're part of a different club, all determined to achieve the ultimate goal… Liam MacCarthy. When you're in there with the rest of those players, fellas from the same clubs aren't cosying up to each other and keeping to themselves, and I have to wonder has that been an issue in some of our neighbouring counties over the years?

It takes some doing to bring 30 lads together from eight-to-10 different clubs and not only create a successful environment, but to keep them united. Every clubman in the county is singing off the same hymn-sheet when you're wearing the county jersey.

And that's been huge for Kilkenny.

We're literally next door to the Shamrocks and there's no point saying otherwise, they're a phenomenal club and you could only admire them. And it's not as if they've a huge parish. Old Kevin Fennelly it was, who brought Knockmoylan, Ballyhale and Knocktopher together, and from the time they merged, they've driven on and won title after title. Back in the 50s, a lot of lads from Knockmoylan used to hurl with Carrickshock.

Lord of mercy on Bob Aylward, but he captained Carrickshock on a couple of occasions to win county titles but that was within the rules at the time… in an era when the parish rule didn't apply. But there's no club anywhere in the country to compare to the Shamrocks. They're so driven.

And when a club maintains such a level of success, that definitely makes it a lot easier to hold onto young, talented players. We've just got to keep plugging away.

★★★

RICHIE JNR

IT'S NOT AS if I'll ever be completely 'gone' from Carrickshock.

Ruairí is hurling for The Village, but Richie Óg will hurl for Carrickshock – 100 percent, and whether it's been involved with his group when the time comes, or older underage panels, I'll never be completely separated from the club. In management terms, I'm young, so who knows, I could very easily end up managing the adult team again at some stage in the future.

My dad is as committed to the club now as he was in his heyday as a player, and mam is as passionate about hurling as she was when she was playing camogie herself, so the bar has been set pretty high for me.

But those are footsteps well and truly worth following in.

★★★

RICHIE SNR

WE ALL ADMIRED how good some Munster Championship matches can be, but during the 80s, Kilkenny, Wexford and Offaly had some great battles in the Leinster Championship. For most of those years, there was only a puck of a ball between the three of us.

In 1985, I was centre-forward against Offaly in the Leinster semi-final and we were nine points up with 15 minutes to go, yet by the call of the match, Offaly had dug out an equaliser. Three weeks later, they beat us in the replay by six points, and went on to win the All-Ireland. Those were tremendous games and it was great to be part of them.

And you can't forget Laois had a serious outfit at the time, and they reached the one-off Centenary Cup final in 1984. It was a seriously strong period for Leinster hurling and whoever walked off with the Bob O'Keeffe Cup was generally always in the shakedown for the All-Ireland title.

We won back-to-back in that decade, something only Galway did as well during the 80s, so all in all, we held our own.

Offaly's success in both codes was, by any standards, a phenomenal achievement. Football in Kilkenny, as everyone knows, is in a poor place compared to other counties, yet I've always loved it… and Matt Connor was a God to me. I'd sit down and watch him play all day, and to end up in a wheelchair at the age of 24 after a car crash on Christmas Day, 1984, was so tragic.

I had a cup of tea with Matt in Tullamore while we were working on this book and it's always good to see him. There's not many in any era who scored 2-9 against Kerry in the championship and to think he did that on a losing Offaly team in the 1980 All-Ireland semi-final.

He was some talent.

Kilkenny's relationship with inter-county football pops up in debates from time to time. But I don't think we're big enough to be in a position to be truly competitive in football given the size of the county in club terms, and our traditional preference for hurling. We've 12 senior clubs and 12 intermediate clubs out of a total of 41 clubs at all grades.

Cork's total club number is 259, Dublin has 134, Wexford has 93, Galway has 80, Tipp has 72. There's no escaping the fact that, in club terms, we're a small county, so to have achieved the way we have when it comes to senior hurling is extraordinary. As a county, we're just not big enough to try and play the two codes with the pedal to the floor, and I say that as someone who loves football... the Mayo team in particular, and I've watched matches all over the country. Hurling is such a skilful game, that if you don't really work at it during the summer months, you'll lose some of your technique.

Then of course there's Offaly, who've achieved such great success in both codes – and that's a county with 61 clubs. They deserve massive credit for what they've achieved in hurling and football over the last 40-plus years. I started travelling through Offaly in the early 80s, through the job, and I have been meeting the likes of Martin Furlong on a fairly regular basis. In 1999, they became the first county to win All Stars in every position in both hurling and football, which is some achievement. That Offaly side we hurled against in the early 80s was a brilliant team and we'd some great battles with them.

ABOUT A FORTNIGHT before the 1985 All-Ireland final, the doorbell rang and who was at the door... only Dermot Healy, who was training Offaly at the time. 'Richie, might you do me a favour?' he said.

'We have no field to train in Offaly at the moment because of the weather (the summer of 1985 wasn't too far removed from the summer just gone) so we're coming to Nowlan Park next Sunday to play at half three... the same time as the throw-in for the All-Ireland the following week... and we're hoping to make it a full 15 on 15 game.

'Could you help us out?'

It was a novel suggestion... to tog out for an All-Ireland hurling final warm-up in Nowlan Park, and Kilkenny's championship done with. But to give our then county board its due, they were delighted to assist another Leinster county like this.

So, there were, I think, six of us, including myself, Kieran Brennan, Joe Hennessy, Harry Ryan, Lord of mercy on him, headed into Nowlan Park for what turned out to be 70 ferocious minutes of hurling. Now, Nowlan Park, at that time, was the only available playing surface in our own county given how bad the weather was.

And once the ball was thrown in, absolutely no-one held back, but that's what Dermot had looked for in the dressing-room beforehand. He wanted a physical, competitive game of hurling and that's what was served up. I was marked by Ger Coughlan and we'd have been familiar with each other from Kilkenny-Offaly matches, and I'm pretty sure we were in the black and amber that day… since the 'first' Offaly team were wearing their own jerseys.

Prior to the match, the Offaly management had their team picked for the final against Galway but there was a change made purely on the basis of the game played in Nowlan Park, when Nick Bermingham, who had played at centre-forward, was dropped. In what was the 99th All-Ireland senior hurling final, Offaly got the better of Galway by 2-11 to 1-12. So, there was some welcome assistance from Kilkenny to our friends in Offaly in the build-up to that All-Ireland win through a Nowlan Park training match, long before pre-All-Ireland sessions in that ground became such a well-known part of our success under Brian Cody.

I WAS CHAIRMAN of the club in 1985 and '86, and I ended up being the only Kilkenny man to win an All Star in '86. What I put into those two years was phenomenal, I don't mind admitting… because I was below in the field as often as I could on account of being chairman of the club and I probably trained harder in '85 and '86 than I did in the previous years and in the years that followed.

I trained with the club on the nights I wasn't training with the county, so I was in great shape in 1986 and everything went really well for me… and an All Star followed.

The fact that I was chairman of Carrickshock at the same time made it all the more special because I was committed to the club and the county equally. I couldn't have done both only for Ann's backing and I'm very proud of that All Star. I got a real kick out of that one, given how busy that year was for me.

No-one else wanted the chairman's job at the time and I ended up giving three to four nights every week of the summer training. I was on the road as well, repping, and it was never a 40-hour week… it was often in the mid-50s, but you just had to do what you had to do. It was a phenomenal year for me, even if we fell short in the championship, losing to Galway in the All-Ireland semi-final (4-12 to 0-13) having beaten Offaly in the Leinster final.

I'd be no different to Richie when it comes to individual awards.

They're nice, don't get me wrong, but they were never an ambition of mine when we'd start back into training at the start of a new campaign. These awards are there at the end of the year and if you're after having a good year and you're lucky enough to firstly be nominated, and then secondly to win, it's a lovely acknowledgement. I was lucky enough to win two of them, but I'd no burning desire for individual honours like that.

If I'd trade my inter-county success for an intermediate medal with the club, then I'd exchange the two All Stars I won in 1982 and '86 for All-Ireland medals in '87 and '91… in a heartbeat. Did the Carrickshock panel need a psychologist to get that extra five to 10 percent out of us? The commitment from the panel was absolute and I still wonder about how we didn't put together the results I felt our effort deserved.

But it's nice to be still around to look back on it, and recognise the enjoyment that so many of us got out of the game.

As far as I'm concerned, the club is everything. It's where I started.

I just love it. It's part of the fabric of this parish. I've been involved in running the club's golf classic for 38 years. I've given a lot of time to Carrickshock but it's time that I've given gladly. I've always had a fierce love for the club and I'm very proud of my unbroken service as player, selector, manager and administrator. I've probably trained every team from under-13 up at different stages with the club. We won a double-double at under-16 and under-18 at Roinn 'A', the only time we ever won anything at that level and I took huge satisfaction from that, given the way that we developed players. Jimmy Sheehan and myself would have put massive hours into that.

We had a great Bord na nÓg group too; my brother, Maurice, John Barron, Seamus Farrell, Stephen Rice, Jimmy Dwyer and Georgie Power. That was a group of us there that worked really hard with those young lads to try and get the very best out of them. I moved up with them then to under-21, and that was a mistake on my behalf. I thought we were good enough to win an under-21 Roinn 'A' but maybe lads get a bit fed with the same face after a while. I always regretted taking on that job – but on the whole, there's not been too many other regrets throughout all my years in hurling.

But at the start of 2023, aged 66, I took on a selector's role with our minor team. Will I ever learn? But do you know what… the fun and the enjoyment is still there. My outlook on hurling at this stage of my life is all about developing players. Country clubs are never going to be massively successful in winning trophies, but if you can develop a group of players at that level and get the skill levels and the right attitude into them, to have them as prepared as possible before they get to adult hurling, that'll be a job well done.

If you can win along the way, brilliant. But there has to be a sense of fun about it. We can't lose sight of that.

Davy Franks, who'd be well known through his coaching role with Ballygunner in recent years and all the success they've enjoyed, is now managing our minor team and I think he's excellent. He's a great way about him and he's moving with the times. I know from the feedback that I get from the Waterford clubs, that he's fierce well thought of and sure they love him in Ballygunner.

It's fantastic for our club to have Richie managing our intermediate team, then you have Davy with the underage team – men with huge hurling experience. I don't think we really appreciate that we have these two guys working with our players. John Tennyson was involved last year with the under-15s and he's another huge addition to the club from a coaching perspective. John has three small kids so he just couldn't do it this year and I understand 100 percent why he couldn't do it. I know down the road, he'll be a lad that will drive on the club for a number of years because he's got a great way about him too.

When lads give eight, 10 or 15 years hurling with the county, that's a massive amount of time and you take in so much, and it's great that so many of these lads have come back to work with the club again. It says a lot for us as a club that they've done so, to be honest. I've seen it myself over the years, that you would have lads who cut ties completely with the club once they finish their inter-county careers. We're very lucky to have retained so many prominent former players as coaches.

Winning the club All-Ireland in Croke Park was such a special night for Ann and myself; it was brilliant because we had the three of them, Richie, John and Jamie, all involved and all making such a huge contribution. I know myself that the group of players that Richie hurled with will wonder how they didn't get over the line in a senior county final. Sure, the same applied to my team not winning the intermediate title.

But you have to stay going.

And you have to put it in context. It isn't life and death, despite what the most ardent hurling supporter might otherwise suggest. Living your life well and being good to yourself and those around you, I'll say it again… that's worth more than any medal.

★★★

SUZANNE

THE CLUB MEANS the world to dad and Richard, and they've always said they'd give up their medals with Kilkenny for a senior title and an All-Ireland with Carrickshock. I think they know how admired they are within the club, not that they've ever made much of that publicly or even at home with us. They're such down to earth people; as far as they're concerned, they're just paid-up club members like everyone else and they just want to give something back… given all the club has done for them. There's nothing either of them wouldn't do for Carrickshock.

★★★

RICHIE SNR

ANN PUT MASSIVE, massive hours into the lads. Once Jamie was there, Richie was there, then Stephanie, it was all go with hurling and camogie – and then along came John and Suzanne… and Ann kept going. I was working long hours on the road and then I was working part-time as well. So, herself had a huge part to play in their involvement in sport, driving them here and there.

When you're on the road, it's not a 40-hour week, it could sometimes be anything up to 60 hours. Bearing that in mind, it was huge that Ann had such an interest in hurling; she'd have spent a lot of nights on her own because I was working part-time as well, trying to build a house and get us on a steady footing as a family.

Now, I was still at hand, going to matches with them and then doing a bit of training for a year or two, but I have to give Ann massive credit. She has as big an interest in it as myself, and we had great times watching the lads grow up, developing their hurling in the garden, off the gable end of the wall… the odd argument being had, and the odd window being broken! And when I look back on it now, the time and effort that we put in… it was well worth it.

We would have struggled financially; the fact that you were trying to live on one wage with five kids, but that was a decision that Ann and myself made, and she put every spare minute she had into the lads.

It worked out great.

II

Sharpening
the Blade

★★★

'It's a game that requires a lot of practice; the finer points and the real skills can only be learned the hard way. I remember when I was a youngster myself, we could spend all day on Sunday in the field, maybe until darkness fell, breaking only for meals. Of course, there were few rival attractions then. Young people hadn't cars, the era of the showbands and big dance halls hadn't come upon us and we hadn't a lot of pocket money. Hurling was everything.'

Jimmy Langton
The Hurling Immortals by Raymond Smith (1969)

★★★

RICHIE SNR

I FIRST PLAYED for Kilkenny at under-14 level in a tournament that pre-dated the foundation of the Tony Forristal Tournament, and all the major hurling counties took part in… Cork, Tipp, ourselves and so on. We ended up in the final, which was played in the Davin Park in Carrick-on-Suir… and we won, which was very satisfying. Carrick was only over the road from our home place so that made it extra special for me.

Back in those underage hurling years, I wasn't rooted into one position. In the 1975 minor championship, I played in three different positions for Kilkenny… wing-forward, centerfield, and in the All-Ireland final against Cork, which we won by 3-19 to 1-14, I played corner-back which was very unusual.

The lad who had been corner-back in the Leinster final, and we'd go on to play side-by-side at senior level, was Christy Heffernan… but he was dropped completely off that minor panel, which I thought was fierce harsh on him. This broke up the midfield partnership I had with Josie O'Brien, the Lord have mercy on him. God, I'm after saying that a good bit, thinking back on the lads I played with against. There's no greater thief than time and you can't help thinking that when you're stood in the graveyard after someone you shared a pitch with has been buried.

But that was the only time I ever wore a back's jersey for Kilkenny; I'd have played a few times at centre-back with the club.

My preference was always to be in attack and I loved the number 11 jersey. I never felt like I was going to be one of those free-scoring forwards, whereas contesting for and winning dirty ball was more my cup of tea. I ended up scoring four points from play as a right-half forward in the 1982 All-Ireland final, which was a huge thrill. That was a very satisfying day. I genuinely didn't mind which jersey I was given. It all boiled down for me like this… if you were prepared to work hard, then you had a chance.

The odd thing about being a forward in hurling is that you spend most of a match with your back to the target, so it's probably no surprise now that you see backs surging forward the way they do currently, both contributing and setting up scores. It's interesting to see how many forwards can convert themselves into quality backs, but it rarely applies the other way round at inter-county level. That in itself shows you what's required to be an effective forward, be it in my own era or when it comes to anyone playing right now.

I think it took me a good few years to build up a sense of confidence, both about myself and in terms of what I could do. For a while, I had it in my head that if someone was going to be taken off, that I'd be first one hauled over the white line. I don't know if that was because I'd come from small club, but that thought definitely lingered for a while.

★★★

ANN

WE BOTH KNEW exactly who the other person was when we started going out, which was obviously a big help to the two of us. We were both mad about the game, so we were a good match… right from the start.

★★★

RICHIE JNR

ST KIERAN'S COLLEGE played a huge role in my hurling education, as it has for so many players both before and after me. The standards there, in many ways, mirrored what was coming down the line for me as a senior hurler with Kilkenny, not that I knew that at the time.

We used to do park runs at lunchtime every Monday and Friday, and I used to hate those sessions. I was always at the back of the group. Tom Hogan, the teacher who was coaching us at the time, used to always run with me at the back because he knew that if he went up to the front, I'd finish the run... but I'd finish it at my own pace.

So, Tom ran with me to push me that little bit harder. He looked out for me throughout my time in Kieran's and we had some great successes the whole way through, winning two Croke Cups, while losing another final, my first, in 2002.

I summed up the culture of Kieran's to Michael Verney in an *Irish Independent* interview in 2016:

'When I was there, I was on the ball wall every single day of the week. You were just looking forward to getting out with the hurl, it was what you lived for in Kieran's.

'The minute the 11 o'clock whistle goes... you're out for the 10 or 15 minutes, and it's the same with the one-hour lunch. You had the hurl in your hand so often, you were perfecting the skills without actually realising what you were doing.

'You were spending at least five hours a week pucking around with the lads, and that's completely separate from the training you're doing. Over six years, that adds up to a hell of a lot of hours and I developed most of my hurling in Kieran's to progress with Kilkenny...

'That's what makes Kieran's so special, their academics is phenomenal but on the sporting side, the teachers just have a love of sport in general. And buying into that mentality at such a young age really prepares you for your future with the game at a high level.'

★★★

TOM HOGAN

(Teacher and mentor, St Kieran's College, Kilkenny)

RICHIE'S TALENT WAS obvious from a very early stage at Kieran's.

We saw the same thing when it came to the likes of Cha Fitzpatrick and Richie Hogan too; they came in as stars in many cases, and left Kieran's as even bigger ones having improved and done so well for us. Richie was undoubtedly one of those star performers.

Before he came into us, we'd have heard talk about Richie Power from Carrickshock being a different kind of hurler from his father and him being much more confident in his own ability – but not in a cocky way, mind you… he was very self-assured. In his first year, he got onto the juvenile team, and from there he progressed onto the junior, minor and senior teams… and he took it all in his stride. You could say it's in the genes when you consider his cousin, Eoin Murphy at the moment and, of course, Richie's own son, Ruairí, who's now in Third Year, is another good prospect.

I'm also involved in cross-country running in the school and myself and John O'Keeffe used to bring the hurlers down to the Castle Park in Kilkenny twice a week at lunchtime as part of the early season work, just to build up a bit of stamina. Richie wasn't too fond of that stuff, but he still did it. Hurling was like a genetic thing to him.

He just wanted to be a hurler. Hurling was more important than academics or anything else. It was his be-all and end-all, and he knew what he had to do if was going to make it. You have to get on to some fellas to get the best out of them, but Richie wasn't one of those fellas. He responded much better to a bit of praise.

He was very good, and from time to time we had to massage his ego a bit to get through to him, but he responded very well to that and we got more out of him through that approach. When you reminded him of how good he was and what we wanted him to do, he went off and did it.

I had Richie as a juvenile in First and Second Year, during which we won two Leinster Championships. He was part of a very good group from Carrickshock, who were winning everything up to and including minor Roinn 'A' the time – Michael Rice, John Tennyson, John Murphy and so on… they were all very good. Shamrocks, with Cha and Michael Fennelly, were very strong at that stage too, but couldn't get the better of Carrickshock in the underage finals. But they turned that around at senior level and Carrickshock somewhat fell by the wayside at the same grade.

Having won two juvenile Leinster titles and one junior title, Richie moved into the senior team in 2002 and played in goal in the Croke Cup final against St Colman's. During the Leinster final, we realised we'd have to make a change in goal beyond that match to give ourselves the best possible chance. It was a big decision but one we felt we had to make, so we put Richie back in goal.

We realised it was going to dent our forward power, but still, we had Cha and Eoin Reid up the field, and we had to do what we felt would give us the best possibility of winning the game. Playing Richie in goal might have cost us an All-Ireland, but without him in goal, we felt we just wouldn't have been competitive in the game the way we needed to be. And we ended up losing by a point.

Richie accepted the decision even though, from the perspective of being such a good forward, he was losing out. He said he'd do whatever was asked of him but he never complained about the decision, and just got on with things. He played very well in goal but, unfortunately, we came up short. Richie had a great pair of hands and a great eye for the ball, and he always wanted the ball... not every player is like that.

He just wanted the ball the whole time. He had great positional sense and he always knew where he should be. Between himself, John and Jamie, there was a huge amount of hurling going on at home and it showed when they all played for us.

Richie just lived for hurling. He boarded in his Leaving Cert year in 2004, which was the last year of boarding in Kieran's. He wasn't the most studious of students, and I know he won't mind me saying that. But he was never any trouble in class; he did what he had to do, academically speaking.

He came into a Kilkenny team that was full of stars but he had great strength, as well as huge skill levels. He had a great pair of hands, left and right. He was willing to catch a ball and had great spatial awareness about where he, and his teammates around him, should be. He was a great man to shorten the hurl to make sure he wouldn't be hooked and he was a great man to get his team a goal with a little wristy flick.

Richie was part of a great era. Michael Rice was the captain in 2002 and he was, I think, the best fella I ever dealt with. He'd ask you what you wanted him to do, and he just did it exactly. Whereas Richie was just a kind of consummate hurler, he just went out and hurled his stuff. He didn't care about the opposition, he just went out and hurled, which was a great attitude to have.

Between the club and the school, he was part of a culture where everyone playing wanted to wear the Kilkenny jersey and that brought the best out of all those lads, and Richie was among the players that shone brightest.

ENDA McEVOY

(Journalist, author and doyen of Kilkenny sportswriters)

IN THE 2002 Croke Cup final, St Colman's of Fermoy beat Kieran's (by 0-11 to 2-4) on a very windy day in Semple Stadium. Kieran's had been leaking goals in the campaign up until then... Richie went back from the forwards to goalkeeper, and he solved the problem for two reasons.

One, he was the best goalkeeper in the school and his reflexes were brilliant; and two, he ended playing as a sweeper-keeper. Richie cleaned up everything. He was like an auxiliary full-back and everything that needed to be stopped... he stopped. And he cleaned up everything behind the full-back line and was firing the ball 90 yards down the field. It was certainly a case of robbing Peter to pay Paul by repositioning Richie for the final but it just underlined how big a talent and how excellent a reader of the game he was.

The 2003 final was played in Clonmel, when Kieran's took on Colman's again, winning comfortably on this occasion (by 1-15 to 1-4) with Richie restored to the attack. Limerick's Andrew O'Shaughnessy was Colman's outstanding player at the time, so you had two of the country's best underage hurlers at opposite ends of the field.

It was another windy day, and Kieran's had the wind in the first-half. They won a couple of frees that were 40 yards out and Richie took them in a way that didn't occur to anyone else that day. He skimmed both of them just over the crossbar.

He was basically aiming for the roof of the net, hoping to sneak one in. So, if the ball didn't go in, it was going to go over... it's just not something you'd see a teenager usually doing, something as sophisticated at that.

ANN

RICHARD'S CAREER WAS like the stuff of dreams. And he was cocky out from his teens. I remember him outside Kieran's College, telling his father he'd have to do Transition Year because if he didn't, he'd be doing his Leaving Cert when he'd be hurling minor for Kilkenny… and it was well and truly a case of when… not if!

His cards were marked pretty early in terms of where hurling would end up taking him, but none of us could have seriously thought he'd end up with eight All-Ireland medals before he was even 29 years of age. He was a very talented player and, putting the disappointment of retiring so early to one side, it was some career at the same time.

And he wore having the same name as his father fairly lightly.

★★★

RICHIE JNR

AFTER I ANNOUNCED my retirement from inter-county hurling, all sorts of thoughts ran through my mind. *Did the knee problems really begin back when I was 15, when I'd had my first operation and then played in a colleges' All-Ireland final four weeks after that procedure?*

Was that the start of it all? Was it a case of me pushing myself too hard?

Did I do things right by the knee, going right back to the first injury?

Should I have taken a year out from hurling when I was in Kieran's?

These are all unanswerable questions now, of course, but I will always look back on my time at Kieran's with huge affection.

★★★

RICHIE SNR

WHEN RICHIE WAS around 12 or 13, you could see the talent starting to emerge. He had tremendous vision on the ball and he was never in any way selfish.

It didn't matter who got the score, once his team scored, that's the way he was thinking. I was heavily involved with him at under-14, 16 and 18, and there were probably times when I'd have been hard on him, but all the while, the quality of Richie's play shone through. He was good in the air, and he had a great awareness of space all around him when it came to distribution.

His vision was what stood out to me from a very early stage.

There were eight to 10 young lads in the club around the age of 16 who were really emerging as good hurlers. They stood out a mile. I always felt that by the time they were 19 or 20, at least four of them were certainties for the Kilkenny seniors… Richie, John Tennyson, Michael Rice and John Dalton. And there were great players emerging elsewhere in the county at the same time, like Michael Fennelly, Cha Fitzpatrick, Eoin Larkin and Willie O'Dwyer.

Richie gave three years at minor and three years at under-21 with Kilkenny, that was a huge achievement and a lot of experience gained. But you'd look back on it now and wonder was that workload one of the main reasons he ended up having to call it a day when he did.

He was a starter in every team he played in, so you'd have to wonder about the level of wear and tear on the body. He hurled minor with Carrickshock for five years, was a key man on the Kieran's College team when they won a couple of All-Irelands, and was playing adult hurling at a young age… so you're talking about serious mileage before he'd turned 21.

I always thought I was fair when it came to training my own three lads with the club. Sure, you had to be fair, I didn't know any other way. Ann would maintain that I was probably too hard on our lads, but I don't think I was.

At that particular stage, we were competing in Roinn 'A' which the club had never done. We were lucky enough to win two county under-16s and minor titles, which was massive for the club. Those wins were the foundation of our intermediate and senior teams for 10 to 15 years after that.

To have that many young lads from the club following on from myself and Pat Dwyer, and being selected for Kilkenny was huge at the time. Never in our wildest dreams did we think we'd have four lads playing minor with Kilkenny at the same time, and then going on to under-21 and senior… and all the All-Irelands that came their way. The enjoyment we got out of seeing our own lads making such a contribution to Kilkenny's success for about 15 years was huge.

Going all the way back to the Tony Forristal tournament, which Jamie and John played in as well as Richie, it really was some era.

But look, it's a difficult one to balance.

I honestly believe that my lads had to be treated the same as the other 22 or 23 on the panel. Looking back on it, there were times maybe I might have been hard on them in matches. But most managers never intentionally to go out and deliberately criticise anyone.

The biggest quality that you need on the sideline is a bit of coolness and calmness. I sometimes get sucked into a game, and when you're young, and when you're mad to win and you've trained so hard to win, it's hard to stay calm at all times.

But I was like that when I was hurling myself. I tried to keep level-headed the whole way through.

By the time he was 18, it really did feel like it was only a matter of time before Richie stepped up to senior hurling with Kilkenny. He had this way of doing things. You might even say at times that he might have been overly involved in looking for other players but, to me, it was his real strong point from a very early age.

It just came naturally to him. Sometimes you may have to bring lads into a training ground and work on that and get lads to do it – to look for someone in a better position, and put a teammate through – but it just came so naturally to him.

III

For Whom the Bell Tolls: Injuries and Acceptance

★★★

'Happiness is in many things. It's in love. It's in sharing. But most of all, it's in being at peace with yourself knowing you are making the effort, the full effort, to do what is right. True happiness comes from the things that cannot be taken away from you. Making the full effort to do the right thing can never be taken away from you. I believe the greatest joy one can have is doing something for someone else without any thought of getting something in return.'

John Wooden from *'Wooden: A Lifetime of Observations and Reflections On and Off the Court'* (1997)

★★★

RICHIE JNR

FOR ALL THE injuries I'd had up to that point, I could never have imagined being told that my inter-county career would be over aged 29. Nothing lasts forever, we all know that, but at the end of the 2015 All-Ireland final, I genuinely felt I might have two, even three good years left in me at that level.

It was way too early in my mind to be thinking about daisy pulling and cheering for Kilkenny above in the stand as a civilian.

I came on as a sub in that final for the last 12 minutes, replacing Richie Hogan; John came on the same day a few minutes after me for Ger Aylward. I was surprised I even made the panel that day because that whole year, personally, felt like a massive waste. Mentally and physically, it was probably the toughest year I ever put in when it came to hurling, even taking in everything else I'd gone through, on and off the field, up to that point.

WHEN 2014 HAD ended on a high for me, I was looking forward to driving on, being match fit and ready to make my contribution.

That year, I started the first game in the championship against Galway in Tullamore; I did the posterior cruciate in my knee that day and that put me out until the All-Ireland semi-final against Limerick in an absolute monsoon in Croke Park, when I came on as a sub. By the time I went in at full-forward, the jersey felt like a 10-stone weight on my back with all the rain that was after falling by then.

There's not been a match played in that kind of downpour at Croker since. We might have ended up winning by six points but it never felt in any way comfortable; Limerick threw everything at us and made us work the whole way down the stretch. I did enough in the eyes of Brian Cody to get back into the starting team for both the first match against Tipp, and the replay. I was 27, going on 28, at that stage and I was after getting myself into good shape.

I'd worked with a personal trainer for the first time that year and things had come together really well. I felt like I'd laid a foundation for another few years with Kilkenny on the back of that work. I'd put some distance between myself and the off-field issues, and I felt like I was in a good place.

We regrouped for our first 2015 training session out in Dunmore, and we were playing a possession game towards the end of training. It was the very last ball of the night, someone was coming at me... and I went to meet him with a shoulder.

But whatever way he side-stepped me, my body went one way and my left leg stuck in the ground. The first thought was that I'd done the cruciate again.

Thankfully, it didn't turn out to be that; it was a cartilage problem instead. But it marked the start of a year from hell for me, because from that January, the whole way through to the All-Ireland final, I was never right. I think I hurled one game with Kilkenny that whole year... the Jamie Wall fundraiser in Cork, but I just couldn't get the knee right.

And in the space of nine months, I ended up having four knee operations. I've had six altogether, so to have four inside a year was hard going. Very hard going.

The first three (surgeries) dealt with the cartilage; keyhole jobs which got in there and cleaned it out, and to have a look at what was going on in there – and that was grand. But no matter what rehab, or how much of it I was doing, and despite doing all the right things off the field, the knee still wasn't coming right.

The whole thing drained me.

WHEN YOU COME out of the dressing-room in Nowlan Park, there's two directions you can travel: left for the gym, or right onto the field. That year, every single night I was going left… while the lads were going right, and I spent a lot of those nights on my own in the gym. Now, there'd have been times when other lads would have been having picked up injuries, but never for night after night the way I was.

You'd be hearing the lads out on the field urging each other on, or looking for a ball when they'd be playing a game at the end of a session and, all the while, I was in the gym, doing all I could to be back out there with them, and stuck in the middle of it all. Our physios, Kevin Curran and John Kearns were the most regular other people in with me, advising me as best they could, but a lot of what I had to do, I was doing on my own and there was no fun in it.

It was like being in a vacuum.

At one stage that year, I went to Brian – and Tadhg Crowley, our team doctor, was there at the time as well – and I was almost in tears.

'Something's not right!' I said to them.

'And how can it not be right at this stage; I've done everything that's been asked of me.' The surgeon, Tadhg O'Sullivan, had told me that he'd gone in and had a look at the knee itself, and said there was no debris there, and that it looked okay.

But I kept doing my rehab; sure, I'd no option, let's face it.

I wanted to be back hurling and I knew what I had to do. I just had to hope that it'd all pay off down the line for me and, around the time of the All-Ireland (final), things started to come right… I think I trained once or twice.

My fitness wasn't bad… I was doing a lot of fitness work in the pool with Mick Dempsey to keep up my aerobic fitness. but I'd done very little hurling. In the lead up to the final, I didn't expect to be on the 26, as the whole year up to that point had been a total disaster from my point of view for both club and the county.

But, lo and behold, I ended up on the 26… and got the last 12 minutes.

Tadhg O'Sullivan had told me that when the county season and the club season was finished, that he was going to go back in and do whatever needed to be done. So, I hurled the All-Ireland and then went back to the club. There were two weeks between the All-Ireland and the first round of the senior championship in Kilkenny, and we were playing first round relegation: so if won, you were in a quarter final, and if you lost you were in a relegation final.

And I remember going down to Tadhg O'Sullivan the Friday before that game and he took three syringes of fluid off my knee, and injected me with a painkilling injection just to get through the game, which was grand. So, I got through the game, which we lost and, two weeks later, I went down to Waterford again, got fluid taken off the knee again and got another injection.

We were beaten in the relegation final by St Martin's (2-13 to 0-13) at Nowlan Park, which was naturally a disappointing way to end 2015. I was really struggling by then; I'd been literally taping myself up to get through games for the club.

Now maybe a lot of lads having the same trouble with the knee wouldn't have bothered, but I know I played a lot of games with the club when I wasn't 100 percent fit and I don't regret it, because I feel you have to give more back to your club than you do in an inter-county set-up. At the end of October, Tadhg said he was going to go into the knee and have a look – and there was a mention of a microfracture, a procedure that's done on damaged knees.

I'd spoken to Shane Walsh, a respected physiotherapist, about the microfracture and I'd been told that it had a similar recovery period to a cruciate (procedure), but not quite as long. I asked when could I expect to be back out on the pitch, and I was told that the end of May or early June the following year looked realistic.

So, I spoke to Brian Cody, told him that I'd be getting operated on, followed by six to seven months of rehab and, at the end of all that, I should be good and rearing to go again. I was turning 29 that December, feeling that I still had two or three years to offer Kilkenny.

Brian was happy enough with that.

I went in and got the operation done and Kathy, my girlfriend at the time, was with me in the room following the procedure. And I was sat there, waiting for the surgeon to come in to do his check before I could go home – it was really just a day procedure.

In he walked, looked at the charts and while these aren't his exact words, in a roundabout way I was told that my playing days were over... that my inter-county hurling career was finished.

All that they could do for me, by that point, was to make me feel comfortable. *Comfortable?*

I was probably still a little bit drugged up at the time and I remember sitting in the bed; the surgeon walked out of the room and I said to Kathy, 'Did he just say what I think he said?'

She confirmed what had been said… and I started bawling.

So, I had my cry, then got myself together, got dressed and was driving back to my parents' house in Stoneyford. The next thing, I was walking in the door back at home – mam and dad were here – and I sat down next to the kitchen table and I started crying again.

I've never been an easy crier.

I still can't remember the last time I'd cried before that day.

And then I told them… 'I'm finished. It's over'.

THE WHOLE THING was so sudden.

In my head, I was facing into six or seven months of rehab to get myself ready for the championship with Kilkenny the following June or July, when things would be ramping up in Leinster. Brian was happy with this; sure, there were previous years when I'd missed large proportions of the league anyway.

The few days after this bombshell had dropped, I was going around in a daze.

I spoke again to Brian, 'our' Tadhg and a few other guys… and the dust settled a little bit. But all the while, I knew I wasn't happy with the outcome and that I wanted second, third, fourth opinions, and that's what I did.

I went up to Ray Moran in Santry with the scans. But he said that the knee was in a bad way. And while there was a possibility that I could get back playing with the club, my high-level inter-county days were over.

AFTER THAT, AND we're talking November by then, I went to Belfast to meet Chris Connolly, whom I was led to believe was one of the best in his field.

I met him at his practice, he looked through the scans, he saw the damage and then talked through different procedures, one of which included breaking my leg and repositioning the bones in an attempt to take the pressure off the inside of my knee where the damage was. He told me I'd be looking at four to six months in a cast. It felt extreme to me.

I came out of that consultation feeling deflated. It just didn't feel like a route I was willing to go down. We were talking about a large area of damage within the knee. And that led to all sorts of thoughts… *Maybe I shouldn't have got the microfracture.* That involved drilling 16 holes in my knee in an attempt to make the bone bleed, in the hope that the blood clots together as an artificial cartilage which gives you the protection the knee requires, and which gives a bit of cushioning between the bones.

But the area was too large and given the size of that same area, it didn't work.

I was driving past Newry and I rang Brian, and I more or less told him that it's done. I'm finished.

'I'm after seeing this specialist and that specialist, and they're all telling me the same thing.'

We'd a good, honest conversation for about 20 to 25 minutes and there was plenty of laughing as well as talking. Brian and myself wouldn't always have seen eye to eye; there'd have been a few clashes over the years.

So, the county board put together a statement that went out on January 19, 2016, and this is how it went:

'Following the most recent surgery to my knee I must sadly today announce my retirement from inter-county hurling. Disappointing though this decision is, I realise and appreciate the opportunity that I had to play alongside some of the greatest players ever to play the game of hurling and to be part of one of the greatest teams of all time all time managed by the greatest manager of all time, Brian Cody.

'I know also how fortunate I am to be able to look back on so many career highlights including the winning of two Colleges, two Minor, two Under-21 and eight Senior All-Ireland medals, as well as being chosen on the All Stars teams in 2010 and 2011.

'I am deeply grateful to all who helped me during my inter-county career, especially Brian, Michael Dempsey our fitness coach, Dr Tadhg Crowley and all the support team in Nowlan Park.

'I extend a very special thank you to my mum Ann, and dad Richie Snr for their support and encouragement at all times. It was very special for me to emulate dad as a minor, under-21 and senior All-Ireland medal winner.

'I want to acknowledge and thank the teachers who coached me in Stoneyford National School and in Saint Kieran's College, and all who helped me in my club Carrickshock.

'Finally I want to say a special word of thanks to Kilkenny County Board, Kilkenny Supporters club and to all Kilkenny supporters who have been so good to me throughout my career. It has been a truly wonderful journey and while I wouldn't choose for it to end like this I will forever cherish the memories of my time wearing the Black & Amber and I wish continued success to all who play for Kilkenny in the years ahead.'

Brian Cody, like so many others at the time, offered kind words after my retirement went public*: 'A terrific hurler, massively skilful. It showed in the last few years because he was playing through injury, limited – almost close to no serious preparation. He came on in the All-Ireland last year and showed what he could do, but going back to the previous year's All-Ireland, he got two goals and was just outstanding. He made a real difference.*

'A hugely skilful player, athletic, brave… he had everything, really. Unfortunately, injury has put an end to his career, but he's a huge loss to the panel, there's no doubt about that.

'Injury is the one thing everybody wants to avoid, some people are lucky and some people are unlucky. He showed what he could do through injury for years; had he been injury-free, we can only imagine. It's unfortunate.'

I found that time very hard to deal with.

And for the weeks and months after that, I struggled to accept that it was over. I drank more than I normally did, to try and deal with it. I was very moody and I was very angry.

I was very angry about how I had got to this point… about how my knee had been reduced by such a level of damage.

NICKY BRENNAN

RICHIE JNR OBVIOUSLY must have had mixed emotions when he was given the diagnosis about his knee. He would have rightly felt he had another three or four years of hurling with Kilkenny when he got the news. And he's the kind of player that couldn't be easily replaced given his skill, strength and aggression.

Henry Shefflin and Eddie Brennan were very different types of players, compared to Richie. And it's not that they weren't brave players, but Richie was particularly brave and was very difficult to handle as a forward. Shefflin was the spiritual leader on the field and conducted the orchestra, while Eddie flashed in goals from all angles. Richie was often the workhorse who won the dirty ball and was able to distribute it to the other forwards.

His influence in terms of the results of games was very significant and I think Kilkenny supporters would very much recognise him for that. And if you go back to some of the goals Richie got, those scores were key to Kilkenny winning a lot of big matches.

★★★

RICHIE JNR

THE ACTUAL REALITY of my inter-county career being over only struck me was when I went down to Walsh Park, for Kilkenny's first round league match with Waterford in 2016. I brought Ruairí with me; we walked in from the Keane's Road entrance at the 'country end' of the stand, and the stand itself was pretty rammed with people and I decided not to walk down in front of the stand because I could just imagine all the questions people would probably put to me, no matter how well intended they were.

So, we ended up on the bank behind the goal for the match (which Waterford won by 0-14 to 0-10) and I remember these words running through my head at the time:

This is it. This is how it has to be for you, now.

You're here as a supporter… and that's all it can be from this point on.

Your playing days with the county are over.

I hadn't viewed going down to that match with any 'final nail in the coffin' thoughts running through my head – but at the same time, that was the reality for me from a playing perspective. I'd had plenty of years with Kilkenny when I'd have gone to league games having picked up niggly injuries; I'd have gone with Ruairí or the father and sat in the stand watching on… but I'd have been going back in on the Tuesday night to do the rehab with a few other injured lads while everyone else was out training.

Only this no longer applied to me.

No training on a Tuesday… no recovery on a Wednesday… and no training on a Friday really took some getting used to.

We'd had the team holiday in December, the lads had gone back training in January and there I was at home, like a de-mobbed soldier… the uniform forever banished to a wardrobe.

It was a huge shock to the system.

FOR THE LIFE of me, to this day I still can't understand how my knee deteriorated so quickly.

From January to June in 2015, everything was okay, but then from June to October, it just deteriorated. Now was that down to something I'd done wrong?

I'm pretty sure it wasn't because I'd stuck to my rehab. I can't help thinking if I'd been told that January that I needed to take a bit of time off – say, a full year away from hurling – to let the knee heal, then I would have.

I was 28 years of age and hoped I'd have another 10 to 12 years ahead of me at club level at the very least, as well as a few more summers with Kilkenny.

WE'D HAVE BEEN one of the best if not the best looked-after set-ups from a medical point of view… expenses, you name it, if the county board could help you in any way, they did just that.

Ned Quinn, who was the county chairman at the time had even suggested he'd send me to Norway or Sweden for specialised treatment, and they were brilliant in that regard.

But I'd love to sit down across the table with people, and have an honest and frank conversation to try and establish how the knee deteriorated the way it did.

But at this stage, I don't think I ever will.

I suppose it's just something I have to live with now.

When I get up out of bed in the morning, my left knee feels a lot more insecure and even more so on cold mornings… it's bone on bone. So, it's all about managing it and that's all I can do. I was on crutches for three months and then I limped for quite a while after that, which again worried me.

But that's long since passed now, thankfully.

Suddenly, for the first time in my adult life, I had a lot of free time – and it was hard. I found myself going for a few pints on a Tuesday night, and the same on either Wednesday or Friday, heading out to watch a match… and that's the way things were in those first few months out of the Kilkenny set-up.

By the time May 2016 came around, something clicked in me. I was going to try and defy the odds and get back playing with the club, if I could.

At that stage, I was still limping and still in quite a lot of pain seven months after the operation – I was sore every day with it, but at least it wasn't disrupting my sleep too much. I was taking my anti-inflammatories and doing everything that was asked of me, but it was still very frustrating. I was expecting things to get a little bit easier; I thought the pain would have subsided by that stage but it just felt like things weren't getting better for me.

But despite the pain, I got myself back into the club gym and started building up the muscles around the knee, to try and take as much pressure off it as I could.

Tommy Shefflin was managing Carrickshock at the time. At the start of the year, I told him to plan without me, but that I was going to do what I could in the gym, work with the club physio and just see what might possibly happen. The more gym sessions I did, the legs started to get stronger, the pain started to subside and that gave me the determination to keep going.

Those nights in the pub faded like a bad memory and I found myself back in a more familiar and way more satisfying pattern. Don't get me wrong: I was still angry that here I was, at 29, and my inter-county career was over at a time in my life when I felt that more Leinster and All-Ireland final appearances could well have been ahead of me.

But I was determined to get back and give something to the club.

When the inter-county announcement was made, I suppose at that time, in my own head, it felt like I was finished at club level too. I felt like there was no way I was going to be able to get back to a situation where I'd be physically capable of hurling for Carrickshock – and that's what really hurt.

NOW, WITH THE advent of the split season, things are different when it comes to planning out your year at both levels. Any of us hurling for Kilkenny were predominantly inter-county players who went back to hurl matches with the club, while rarely training with your club mates until after the All-Ireland final. And by then, you're in the middle of the senior club championship and if you were lucky enough to go on a bit of a run, you got a few weeks with your own lads and nothing beats that.

So, to find myself aged 29, knowing I was 100 percent out of the running with Kilkenny, I knew I owed it to the club to at least see if I could build myself up again. I mean, there's my brother Jamie, 42 years of age and he's still hurling with the club… and so is Michael Rice, who is heading for 39. It just means everything to put on your own club colours and it's not something you'd be inclined to give up easily.

If the fitness stays good and you avoid major injuries, even if it's junior hurling, sure you'd still want to be a part of that. Nothing beats playing hurling, no matter how good a game it is to watch. To be out there in the middle of things… there's nothing that compares with it.

A musician might admire someone else's skill in an orchestra pit, but players always prefer playing. End of.

Those nights, when I genuinely didn't know if I'd ever play again, the fact that the choice had been taken away from me really, really annoyed me. But I knew I could still choose to find out if I could manage it again or not. Anger had clouded me to that prospect in the first few weeks and months following the county board statement. But the deeper I got into the summer, the pain became less and less of a thing for me and I stopped limping.

By July 2016, I'd reached a point with it where I felt pretty comfortable and was pain free ninety-five percent of the time which, in all honesty, was probably the best I could have hoped for after the operation, one way or the other.

In the days and weeks after the operation, I was told that I'd need a replacement in three to four years' time but here I am at 37, eight years on from the operation and I'm still training in the gym, still playing golf, still coaching… and still able to run around and kick a ball with the young lad – and each of those things feels like a gift to me now when I think about how I felt coming home following the operation.

Once the anger subsided, the clouds started to clear and the bigger picture started to emerge. Ruairí was six years old at the time. I wanted to be able to puck and kick a ball around with him and other children I might have down the line.

IN JUNE 2017, I went to Croatia to see if a stem-cell treatment could regenerate the cartilage, but ultimately that came to nothing. To be honest, I hadn't travelled out there with too much optimism but it was worth seeing if there was something in it for me.

As of February 2023, I've now got twice as long out of the damaged knee compared to the initial diagnosis. As for how much more I'll get out of it?

That really is the million-dollar question.

Just over three years ago, I did get stem cell treatment and that has definitely improved things for me. That, combined with the gym work, has clearly helped. I could stumble someday, get my leg caught and jerk it... and that'd probably be that. I had two bouts of stem cell treatment at Medica Stem Cells in Cork under the watch of Dr Gehad El Bastawisy, who has since opened up his own practice, Regenecare, and the last time I was down to him was in early 2021 when I was having another small issue with the knee, but he sorted it.

For me, the treatment has definitely given me a better quality of life and I'm pain-free now to an extent I could never have thought possible in the spring of 2016. And if I can get another five to 10 years like this, I'll be very happy with that.

THE ONE THING I can't do is run.

Funnily enough, I was never a big fan of running when I was training, but now that I can't do it, the fact that I know I can't head off for a five-kilometre run, I do miss it. During lockdown, I was living in Kilkenny, near the Castlecomer Roundabout and I use to go out with a knee strap on and jog on the grass margin alongside the Ring Road for between four and five kilometres.

At the time, there really was nothing else to do... and I was glad of it, not that I was setting the world alight with my pace or anything like that. It was mainly for the head, but it also got the heart rate up.

But then, I backed away from it because I began wondering, was I doing more damage to the knee? So, I got back into the club gym. I was managing Carrickshock by then and I was the only one with a key... I was in there three or four times a week.

As time moved on, the focus had to fall on managing the knee and, as part of that, keeping the gym work up remains very important. I need to do what I can, for as long as I can to keep pressure off the knee.

I've accepted that I'm going to have a knee replacement but the longer I prolong it for say, another five years possibly, will the knee replacement I'll get by then be more advanced than one I could get right now?

A big thing for me in those first few months of rehab was wondering would I be able to play a game of golf, which thankfully I got back to in due course. And, like dad, I just loved it and we're blessed to have Mount Juliet only down the road from home. But I'm thinking about the rest of my life now.

It's no longer about wondering if I can keep hurling.

And I've not lost sight of the fact that had I been playing in my dad's era and picked up a knee problem then, I'd probably be on my second knee replacement by now.

Everything's relative.

NOT ENJOYING THE previous All-Ireland successes, the way I enjoyed 2014, is a huge regret but I can't change the past. In 2006, when we beat Cork, that was my first senior All-Ireland win and, of course, I can remember the final whistle and the celebrations.

The addiction hadn't fully taken hold of me at that stage.

I was gambling actively by then, but not to the extent of where the following years brought me, and the hole that I ended up digging myself into.

RICHIE SNR

1992 WAS MY last year in a Kilkenny jersey.

I'd played centrefield in the '91 All-Ireland final; well, I started at wing forward, but I gave most of my time in the middle of the field and I ended up on John Leahy; in the years that followed, we became great friends when we were in opposition on the road – John was working for a drinks company and I was working for another, and we got to know each other very well.

In early 1992, I was having huge problems with my groins and I went to Ollie Walsh, our manager, and I told him I was pulling out of the panel. I couldn't get the groins right and I was breaking down far too often. It was probably due to wear and tear over the years.

Strangely enough, when I'd give the groins two to three months' rest, they just came together and I started to train with the club and I was hurling well, and things were going good again. We were playing Piltown in Windgap in a knockout championship match, and it was a big one. Hugginstown, which is the upper side of the parish where I was born and raised, was only a stone's throw from Piltown... so it was a real derby.

The club chairman, Paddy Joe Rohan, the Lord have mercy on him, was standing at the dressing-room door as I was going in and he said to me, 'There's a man here looking at you tonight, so put on a good performance'.

That man was Ollie, God rest his soul... he might just be the most likeable man that's ever been involved in Kilkenny hurling. As things turned out, I hurled well on the night.

The following night, I was inside in the County Hospital and John was after being born, and I was at the bed with Ann and baby John. There we all were, when I noticed Ann focusing on the door.

I looked over my shoulder and who was standing at the door, only Ollie Walsh.

'Richie,' he said, 'Can I see you for a minute?'

I can only assume Ollie had made enquiries into my whereabouts and there he was!

'I want you to come back into the panel,' he said.

I was a little hesitant about going back, but ultimately that's what I did and I gave it my full commitment.

THAT YEAR, THERE'D have been league matches in January and February, and I think it was around March or April when I told Ollie that I was crippled. After training sessions and matches, I used to have to drag myself out to the bed.

There was one training session we did on a Saturday night and my brother and a friend of mine from down the road, Richie Long, they were going to play golf and they called in for me to go with them. I told them I wasn't able to walk out of the room, let alone face 18 holes on my feet... and, sure, they laughed at me.

I was just about able to walk by the wall.

But 24 hours later, the legs came right again and I'd be able to walk and go about my business. But the body was telling me that I just wasn't able for that kind of training anymore. That was a small bit hard to accept, but nothing lasts forever.

We ended up facing Wexford in the Leinster final, which we won comfortably enough (3-16 to 2-9). Ollie put me on at half-time, and I only lasted two minutes.

I broke down immediately.

The groin had gone again.

Ann had gone to the ladies the few minutes I ended up playing. She came back into her seat and whoever was sitting beside her said, 'Richie came on at half-time, but he's gone off injured again'.

Ann missed my last few minutes in a Kilkenny jersey.

So that was it.

★★★

ANN

I WAS A bit of a nervous watcher alright.

I remember Richie coming back for Kilkenny in 1992 as a sub against Wexford. At the time, I used to smoke and I went out behind the stand at half-time for one... which turned out to be two. When I came back, Jamie and a few more people sitting near me said I was after missing Richie. 'What do you mean, I've missed him?'

He came on, pulled a hamstring and he was gone back off. It's funny to think of it now but at the time, I think Richie knew his number was up as a Kilkenny hurler. And that was the last time he wore the black and amber.

His time was up, but he'd had a great run – and we'd two lovely weeks in Tenerife straight after that final.

He'd have loved it if they'd beaten Tipp in '91.

★★★

JAMIE

BEING OLDER THAN the rest of the lads, I'd have a few memories of dad playing. In the 1991 All-Ireland final, when I'd have been 11, he was marking John Leahy and he'd a really good first-half... the two of them used to meet each other out on the road, so that was an interesting match-up. Then in '92, dad came back and was brought on as a sub in the Leinster final against Wexford.

Stephanie was gone down with mam, who having a cigarette at the time. Dad's hamstring went and he was back off after a matter of seconds. Back came mam and I told her dad had gone off injured.

'Don't be telling me lies!' she replied.

I had to get a few lads beside me to convince mam I was telling the truth. And that was the last time dad wore the Kilkenny jersey.

★★★

RICHIE SNR

THE 1992 FINAL turned out to be a tight game, but we got the better of Cork by 3-10 to 1-12. And taking 1982 and '83 into account, that was our third successive All-Ireland final win over the Rebels, who wouldn't lift Liam MacCarthy again until Brian Cody's first year in charge of Kilkenny seven years later.

Pat Aylward was a selector from the Shamrocks in 1992, and Pat and I ended up being selectors with Nicky Brennan in 1996-97 and we're all great friends. But he did say to me after the final, 'We'd love to have brought you on, but the game was so tight.'

I knew when the final whistle went in '92 that it was all over for me at inter-county level. I had my mind made up by then, and it was a decision that I came to myself.

I'd had an unbelievable run with Kilkenny. I was a sub back in 1977, then I missed 1978 and '79… came back in '81, and stayed there through to '92. Those were great years and I enjoyed them all, and being the first player to represent the parish in the Kilkenny senior panel meant a good bit to me as well.

When Ollie asked me to go back, I must admit I wondered was I doing the right thing because it's amazing when you move away from the set-up and the intensity of the training, how quickly you drop a gear. And I definitely felt in those training sessions after I went back, that I couldn't get up to the pace; it felt like I was maybe a half yard or a quarter yard behind the lad I was on. You're coming second to too many balls. I wasn't stupid.

I knew myself that there were a lot of miles on the clock and maybe that was the time to step away. But I stayed in, I remained part of the set-up for the

All-Ireland semi-final and final… I was still a part of the squad and that was important as well. All in all, I was fierce lucky when it came to fitness.

Now I did break my two collarbones early in my career: one of them in an under-21 All-Ireland final, and the other one with the club in a tournament match in Knocktopher. Other than that, I broke a couple of bones in the back of my hand during the 1982 intermediate final, just after Kilkenny had won the All-Ireland title.

I'd a few plates put into the back of my hand until it healed. So that kept me out of hurling until the 1983 National Hurling League final against Limerick in Thurles, which we won by two points (2-14 to 2-12)… when I played half an hour. But on the whole, I was lucky on the injury front. I never had a bad knee or ankle injury, and the hamstrings served me well.

MY LEFT KNEE is giving me a bit of trouble nowadays, but I didn't go through anything like what Richie had to deal with before he was even into his early thirties. Thankfully, he's still able to get around, do his job and go enjoy a round of golf. For things to end for him the way they did and he only 29… he should definitely have had another four or five years of inter-county hurling in him. But I look back on all the hurling he did as a young lad – three years minor, then three years under-21, college hurling… and then straight into the seniors – was it too much going at an early age?

It was non-stop activity. Probably, looking back on it, maybe the foot should have come off the pedal when he was younger. That might have helped, but of course there's no way of telling for sure whether that's what did it or not. And, of course, he came into the Carrickshock adult team at a young age.

Looking back on it now, I'd say if he'd had to take a year out, or if someone had to say to him, 'You're out for a year'… he mightn't have ended up with the knee he has now, but look it's easy to be wise after the event.

There's no doubt that the history books will be kind to Richie given his achievements with Kilkenny at all grades.

IV

Hitting Rock Bottom
and Finding a Way Back

★★★

★★★

JOHN KNOX

THEY DIDN'T JUDGE, they didn't crush, they didn't give out. It was a private thing that Richie had to handle. And he did, he handled it like a man.

He didn't run away and try and pretend, 'Oh, this didn't happen', and it wasn't a case of him not reaching out.

He showed strength of character in the way he went about it.

Mentally, he could have been crushed by it. But that didn't prove to be the case. I don't know what the numbers involved were or anything like that. Kilkenny sport backed off him, because the Powers are so highly thought of.

The first thing someone would have said at the time was to offer a kind word and wish good luck to Richie and the family. He was given space, and he had his own strength of character and family support.

And that family support would extend to Kilkenny GAA, who wouldn't have abandoned him and would have made sure that Richie got what he needed.

The support system was there, be it up front or be it slightly removed, but he was never abandoned. It wouldn't have been the Kilkenny way, in fairness. Sometimes you have to cut people loose but no, the Powers wouldn't have been cut loose, no way.

Did he ever do something that cast a shadow on him or his club or Kilkenny?

No, he didn't.

It was a personal thing that got hold of Richie, and he was given the space and the support, and it's a period of his life that thankfully faded away.

★★★

RICHIE JNR

2013 WAS A bit of an odd championship campaign from a Kilkenny perspective. Looking at it from a wider angle, it was probably the most open championship of my playing career and there hasn't been one like it since.

Dublin beat us in a Leinster semi-final replay in Portlaoise (1-16 to 0-16) and the draw for the qualifiers had already been made… Tipperary six days later in Nowlan Park. I'd been sent off on a second yellow card with about five minutes to go. That was the only time I was sent off in a championship match; I saw the line in a league match only the once too, below in Cork.

I was gutted by the second yellow against Dublin. I didn't feel it was warranted. We were pretty much chasing that game from the throw-in, and it was one of those days when we were always playing catch-up.

Afterwards in the dressing-room, I noticed that there were a few heads down. So, I stood up and, whether it was my place to say it or not, I told the lads, 'Look, it's done. Let's just think about what we're facing in six days' time'.

It was one of those rare moments in my inter-county career when I felt I had to rally the troops. I didn't get up and say those few words on account of being sent off: it was because of what was coming six days later. Someone had to say something, I felt.

The adrenaline was still flowing, so up I got.

A few other lads spoke after me. We were still in the championship. And Tipp focused the mind straightaway.

THE FOLLOWING SATURDAY was a roasting hot evening and the ground was full to capacity, with just over 22,000 inside the gates. The talk was that Tipperary were coming to 'do away' with Kilkenny and that this was going to be the end of our era as the dominant team in hurling. Henry made his first appearance of the summer off the bench, and Eoin Murphy came back in, despite being stretchered off against Dublin with a suspected broken ankle, and produced a brilliant performance. Eoin Larkin was on free-taking duty and did the business for us, while I scored twice from play.

It was a very special night, to take Tipp out of the championship on our patch (by 0-20 to 1-14). Brian Cody said a lot after the match, while saying very little.

'Our form wasn't good coming into to it but we were in our own place and the consequences for losing were absolutely powerful for both teams. We are still alive and have a qualifier match next week. They are men.'

The rivalry with Tipp was huge and we played each other on such a regular basis during those years – six summers in-a-row – and most of those matches were ferocious. Huge occasions. No one in Nowlan Park that evening will ever forget it. I remember we went into the ground about an hour and a half before the ball was thrown in, and we just went out for a walk on the field. And the place was already packed… it was like a cauldron.

The heat was incredible. Clear skies overhead and not a puff of a breeze.

How the f**k are we going to hurl in this? I thought to myself. The atmosphere was ramping up, with Henry was on the comeback trail after the cruciate injury from the previous year, coming on with six minutes to go. Everything was built up; it was like a rocket on a launchpad.

Lar Corbett went off with a hamstring injury after half an hour having started really well, scoring a goal and causing us lots of problems. What way it would have gone if he had stayed on the field, I don't know, but we came out on top and it was a sweet win. It really was one of those great nights.

We were out for the fourth successive weekend the following Saturday in Thurles against Waterford and it was another massive battle; it might even have been the best game of that year's championship. We won by 1-22 to 2-16 after extra time, so we'd come through two massive occasions against two of our neighbours, and then we had a two-week break before playing our old friends from Cork in a quarter-final. But that's where our All-Ireland defence came to an end, losing by 0-19 to 0-14 in Semple. It might well have been the only time there was some level of collective fatigue running into games but that wasn't because we were overtrained or anything like that. It was purely down to playing a capacity of games that we just wouldn't have been used to.

We'd become accustomed to the five-week gap after winning a Leinster final, and we used to go back to our clubs for a week after and play a round of county championship games before the four-week bloc leading up to the All-Ireland semi-final.

THERE WAS A bit of a sideshow in the build-up to the Cork match.

Now this might be the only time anyone has ever described Bruce Springsteen as a sideshow… but here we are. 'The Boss' was playing in Nowlan Park the same day that the two All-Ireland quarter-finals were being played in Cork, and our game should have been the second match of that double header.

But the Kilkenny County Board asked for it to be changed, as board officers needed to be back in Nowlan Park for a few different reasons. This was all going on in the background but we weren't made too aware of it, all we heard were murmurs.

So, we played first, against Cork and maybe it was symbolic of the way the way the year had been for us; we never really hit form against them, but that was probably because Cork didn't allow us. They came at us with everything they had and, of course, Henry was sent off after getting two yellow cards in the first-half (the dismissal was later scrubbed from the record by the Central Hearings Committee) and I had to re-take a penalty which I'd originally scored, only to see it stopped the second time.

Things went against us that day when it came to a few decisions and we felt that referee Barry Kelly was harder on us than he had been on Cork. He was mic'd up that day and we felt he was fairly abrupt. Now Cork deserved their win, don't get me wrong and they ended up losing the All-Ireland final after a replay against Clare. From our end of things, a lot of perspective was added to whatever disappointment we had when news broke about Barry Kelly's wife, Catherine, dying that September after a brief illness, aged just 41, the mother of twin boys who were only three at the time.

And then we lost the county senior final that same year.

2013, even allowing for the league final win over Tipp – also at Nowlan Park – was a tough one to take. Those seasons with one 'what if' are bad enough. To end up having two of them was even harder.

But little did I know that, just around the corner, worse was to follow.

EIGHT DAYS AFTER we'd lost the county senior final to Clara, I was dropped – I suppose you could say, informally – from the Kilkenny panel which would have been headline-making news as far as most people would have been concerned, and set tongues wagging both within and beyond the county.

But there was very little talk about it because it was never really announced. I presume the idea behind that was to leave the door open to me returning.

A conversation was had in Hotel Kilkenny involving Brian Cody, Mick Dempsey, James McGarry and Derek Lyng, sitting around the table with myself.

I was after spending the week on the beer and was severely hungover for most of the previous week. I was actually sitting at home in Stoneyford having Sunday dinner with my parents and family – that was the first proper thing I'd had to eat all week.

The next minute, the phone rang and I saw it was Brian ringing me… and I thought to myself, *Jesus, this is a bit strange*. I'd have rarely if ever heard from him in October.

He said he and the management wanted to meet the following night.

'Grand, no bother,' so in I went.

A conversation was had regarding what was going on off the field with myself on a personal level – the gambling – and I came to the conclusion that they were not keen on having me around the set-up and that I was no longer required on the panel at that time.

But the gate wasn't being bolted shut.

Derek was going to be my contact in the months that followed, so it was up to myself to go away and get myself sorted, both physically and mentally. I knew I wasn't in the best physical shape that I could have been in, but mentally I was just destroyed, *really*.

I was all over the place.

I knew I had a lot of work to do to get myself back on an even keel. But right then, I really didn't know if I'd get to wear the Kilkenny jersey again. But that was only a fraction of what I knew I was going to have to admit to, face up to, and deal with.

IN MARCH 2022, I spoke publicly for the first time about my gambling on *The GAA Social* podcast with Thomas Niblock and Oisín McConville – whom dad and I had driven up to meet – about what I was going through almost a decade previously. It felt like the right thing to do. And this is the thrust of what I told them both.

'I've struggled with a gambling addiction as well. And everything (Oisín) said

rings through for myself as well. It probably started at a relatively young age – around 17, maybe 18 at the time – and it would have been very small at the beginning. And then it just grabbed hold of me as it does and it's affected so many other people as well.

'It's affected me throughout my sporting career.

'Being an inter-county player, you've so much free time. At weekends you're not out socializing, so you're trying to fill that void. I would have used gambling as an escape. It was an escape from me, from the hurling… and from other problems that were going on in my life… injuries, for example.

'Any time I would have broken down injured, it spiralled that way in my own head, thinking…

Do you know what, no-one's going to say anything to me, they're going to feel sorry for me, I feel sorry for myself.

'It just had a huge impact on me personally, mentally and physically as well.

'I was hurling with Kilkenny and all this was going on in the background and you're trying to manifest a life that's perfect and great, whereas in the back of it, you're in complete turmoil and you're fighting with it; knowing as well that I was struggling with an addiction… but not being strong enough to ask for help, not being strong enough to go home and sit down with my parents and family… and (not) being man enough to do that.

'I just tried to hide it and continued on down that long, lonely, dark road until… eventually, I couldn't go any further at the end of 2013. And that's when I was surplus to requirements within the Kilkenny set-up… and probably rightly so, because no manager or coach would want that kind of issue going on or being around the set-up.'

Thomas Niblock: *'And is that why you weren't part of the set-up?'*

'No, I wouldn't blame that. I'd blame a dip in form, a dip in fitness. We were beaten in the senior county final that year as well and I didn't have a good season with my club. I probably didn't have a good year with Kilkenny in 2013 either and obviously with this all going on the background as well.'

Oisín then spoke about meeting dad and myself in the Carrickdale Hotel in Dundalk and he obviously had a deep personal insight into how gambling can disassemble your life, bit by bit.

'Like most people you sit down with for the first time, it all becomes very raw. You go back and you start thinking about where is this person at right now?

'I knew that's where I once was and you start to relate to that because, as somebody

who is in recovery, you can get very frustrated sometimes with people when you hear them saying "I can't get where I want to get to" but you have to bring yourself back and remember how tough it was then.

'Because there's loads of different things going on and, one of the things, just when I was listening to Richie talking, is the confidence that it takes away from you. You talk about false confidence – you go out onto the field and you are the man – and really inside, you are just an insecure, little boy.

'You feel like an impostor.'

★★★

RICHIE SNR

RICHIE WASN'T GOING well at the time and I know myself and herself had discussed it at the table on a good few occasions.

'What's going on' was something we both said to each more than once.

The day after the senior final, we went down to the local and I just wasn't happy: after being beaten, how would you be? I was disappointed and all that, but I kind of sensed that something else wasn't right. I saw people looking at me in a slightly different way than usual and I know most of them were probably thinking, *Your lad didn't go well yesterday.*

But there was still something a bit off, as far as I was concerned. I went to Hugginstown that night and I wasn't comfortable there at all, so I got a taxi back to Stoneyford, went back into the local and sat up with a guy that didn't talk hurling at all, a local businessman called Padraig O'Rourke. He just mentioned it briefly, saying, 'I know you don't want to talk about it'.

I got up the next morning, and I had the day off, but up I got and Ann asked me where I was going? I told her I was going to work. I ended up driving to Tramore and I did a bit of work on the laptop and rang the office and so on.

I then went off for a walk that day and my head was all over the place. I was just in a bad place and I walked as far as I could go, and then I sat down on a seat.

I was all on my own; the match was going through my mind but I just knew that something wasn't adding up. I couldn't have been any lower than I was that day. I knew something was wrong.

This wasn't just about hurling.

I couldn't help feeling that something wasn't right with Richie. I got fish and chips, headed off home… but just couldn't shake off that restless feeling.

I went home and said to Ann, 'Listen, I'm going to get Richie out here on Friday evening. Something isn't right'.

Now I had heard and read a bit about inter-county players gambling but no one had said anything to me about there being a problem close to my own front door. What disappoints me to this day is that surely a few people must have known about it well before it eventually came into wider knowledge. I'd have felt that someone should have come to me, or someone should have known me well enough to sit down and talk about it. Surely someone interacting with Richie on a regular basis within Kilkenny hurling had to have twigged something? And if they did, then why didn't they come to me? They surely knew me well enough to talk to me about this. But no one ever came to me.

RICHIE CAME OUT home to us that Friday night and we sat down at the table, and that was the beginning of getting everything sorted. I just sat at the table and I said to him, 'Now Richie, I'm going to ask you one question… but don't answer it if you're not going to tell me the truth.

'Are you gambling?'

There were tears at the table that night and it all came out.

It wasn't pretty, but it was the start of sorting the problem. Yes, there was sadness that evening but there was relief too.

So, you had the defeat in the senior final, Richie wasn't hurling well; then there was the reaction the few days after it, it all felt like something unhelpful and troubling was gnawing away at me. I'd a sense of total frustration that week.

Before it all came to a head, we'd often have asked him was everything okay? But unless you know with 100 percent certainty, it's very hard to say to someone… 'Listen, you're gambling!'

Looking back on it now, maybe we'd handle it differently, but I could never say at any particular stage that I was really, *really* worried about something like that. For one thing, he was unbelievable with Ruairí; he just couldn't do enough for him.

I remember him coming in from a holiday one year; it was the end of January and we were in the kitchen, we'd had something to eat and I was doing something on the computer and he said to Ann, 'Sure I won't be seen out now 'til Easter'.

He was in the prime of his life... he was maybe 24 or 25 at this stage, and I just said to myself, *Well, that definitely won't happen.* But he never stirred outside the door from that last week of January, until Easter, which that year was sometime in April. So that'll tell you the commitment that he and the rest of the lads on the Kilkenny panel were putting in, and sure most of them probably needed some kind of outlet.

But I just didn't know that there was an issue with gambling.

Maybe we weren't sharp enough.

★★★

RICHIE JNR

LET'S GO BACK to when the problem was at its worst.

Losing the 2013 senior final compounded my turmoil. And to this day, it still haunts me in a way. When we won the intermediate back in 2004, we had a very good team; we were a young group and a lot of people were saying we'd end up being a very good senior team and that we'd hopefully push on to win the senior title – and we certainly held our own.

We ended up in two finals and we couldn't seal the deal in either of them.

In 2010, we went in very naively against O'Loughlin Gaels, who were a well-seasoned team. Both personally and as a team, I think we were a little bit overawed by the occasion itself while on the field, you know; physically we were just bullied and that hurt a lot.

But then we got back to the final in 2013, having beaten Ballyhale Shamrocks in the semi-final who were *the* team to beat, so that was a massive result for us. We went in against Clara who had only won the intermediate the year before, so we probably went in as favourites and we'd put ourselves in a great position to win the game, but we didn't see it out and that was very hard to take.

Then eight days later, being dropped off the Kilkenny panel really compounded things.

Something hit home with me, then. I knew something needed to change.

I LEFT THE meeting, and ended up in Matt The Miller's for another night on the beer again. The following day, the realisation about what happened really kicked in.

I was 26… going on 27, and I'd just been dropped off the Kilkenny team.

I came home and spoke to my parents, and by then they knew my own situation. So, I just had to make a decision. I needed to get this thing under control. No, it was a lot more than that. I needed to get it sorted.

I had to hit rock bottom before I asked for help.

Gambling is like any other addiction out there. Unless you want help and unless you acknowledge that you've hit rock bottom, you're not going to ask for it. Because it's a vicious cycle. There were times when I got so down; looking back on it now, I find it hard to believe now just how down I felt and how serious the whole thing had become. It had overwhelmed me.

It was like a massive wave running on a loop… continuously crashing over me.

THAT TUESDAY MORNING, after the meeting and the beer, that was my rock bottom. The week after the senior final, in hindsight, it felt like the warm-up act to something even worse. Drinking for the week numbed the pain; it numbed reality to be honest, and it really was a vicious seven days.

One night led into the next day …and the day leads into night, and so.

At that stage, sitting at home here, with dad, it really was a case of shit or bust really. I knew the choice I faced: get this thing under control now, regardless of my inter-county career and whatever might come of that.

This was a much bigger thing that I needed to solve.

I needed to sort it out.

Getting my life back on track was more important than ever pucking a ball again. Had I stayed on the road I'd been going down, I'd end up losing everything… family, friends and, above every other consideration, Ruairí, who was only heading for five years of age at the time.

Leaving the Hotel Kilkenny meeting, my head was so f***ing frazzled, and it did get me thinking… *Do I really care that much about hurling for the county?*

Was the decision that had just been disclosed to me the end of the world? Because I knew myself what was going on in the background. I knew where I was.

I knew my life was in turmoil at that stage.

And maybe, this was the kick up the arse that I needed, in a way. When I eventually hit rock bottom, it wasn't about hurling or anything like that. It was all about the future. I had to learn to ride that wave rather than succumb to it.

The consequences of my addiction could have seen me end up in serious financial difficulty, and that could have landed me anywhere... even in a jail cell – who knows?

I knew that something had to give.

Luckily enough, that's when I reached out to the GPA, who were fantastic during the whole thing – and they still are. At that stage they put everything in place for me to go and speak to the right people. Going in and doing a stint in a rehab centre was spoken about at home with mam, dad and the family. But I didn't want to do that, because I knew if I went down that road, it was going to become public knowledge.

Whereas, if you're doing counselling and you're going to your Gamblers Anonymous (GA) meetings, that can be done on a daily or weekly basis without being away from your family, your friends and your job, and that ended up being the route I took.

THE GPA WERE brilliant through it all, got me in touch with a guy in Dublin who I started to see straightaway and I began to go to GA meetings in Dublin, regularly.

And that was how my recovery started.

Now, in saying that, it wasn't all plain sailing, because I did relapse along the way. And until such time as you hand over all power to the recovery program, you're not going to get to where you need to go. I found it hard to do that at the start. But I managed to get back on the horse and get into the habit of doing the right things.

Anyone out there that has had a gambling addiction, and has been in GA for months and years, knows you just have to do the program. You have to just go through the steps.

And once you admit that you're powerless over it, that's the first step really.

It had gotten to that stage where I was nearly wanting to lose. I knew this was damaging me. I knew it could destroy me. So, while something at least began to end in the autumn of 2013, something better had also begun.

I decided to resume training and to get myself into good physical condition, even though getting back with Kilkenny was still way down my list of priorities – but Carrickshock was going to be there for the foreseeable future anyway. Luckily enough, one night in the Hotel Kilkenny gym, I got chatting to Mickey Comerford, who is probably one of my best friends now, but at the time I wouldn't have known him that well.

I obviously would have known he played soccer for Kilkenny City, had represented Ireland, was in the army and very much into his fitness. Having explained my situation to Mickey I asked him to put together a fitness program for me, which he duly did, I started training with him a couple of evenings every week and he was a huge help… we did a lot of sessions in Scanlon Park on the running track, and fitness tests in the Hotel Kilkenny car park.

All the while, through December 2013 and into the new year, I met with Derek Lyng and did a few running sessions with him – he wanted to see where my fitness levels were. Derek might have rung me every second or third week, asking me if I was around Wednesday lunchtime to do a session. I wasn't in frequent contact with him or weekly contact with him. I was literally left alone to my own devices.

I suppose the Kilkenny management's way of looking at it was to see what way I'd react to the whole thing. At that time, I had no communication or contact with Brian or Mick or James, or anything like that. I wasn't part of pre-season with the Kilkenny panel. I wasn't part of the WhatsApp group or anything like that.

I was doing my own thing training-wise and then, away from training, I was going to my counsellor and the GA meetings, and stuff like that. I was trying to get some sort of control back regarding life while obviously working at the same time as well; to try and manage everything the best way possible while not looking too far into the future.

As for Kilkenny, it really was a case of what will be, will be.

The training with Mickey was brilliant, and it got to a stage where we could have been meeting up every day or every second day. We were doing beep tests in the car park of Hotel Kilkenny!

If people had seen me, they would have thought I was mad.

But number one, I had a point to prove to myself.

And then, number two, I probably had a point to prove to Brian (Cody). The switch flicked, definitely, about my mentality when it came to training, and dealing with what was going on with my addiction, and trying to understand it.

I don't think I ever fully understood it, but tried to just get it under control.

I KNOW I'LL always be a compulsive gambler, and that's the reality of it.

Even though I haven't had a bet in years, I know it's still there and I'll always have to work at controlling it. But the madness started to settle.

The fog started to disappear and I could see things a lot more clearly. My daily mood was better, and I'd a bit more of a pep in my step as I moved through February, March and April of 2014. Now there were some slips along the way – less than the digits on one hand, mind you – and there were more than a few triggers, such as when things aren't going great, when relationships go through rough patches, and just that sense of things being a bit of a struggle from time to time.

Gambling isn't even a lifestyle. It just takes over.

It takes over your thought process. Everything that you're trying to do the right way gets engulfed by it, but sticking with the training and having a better handle on things off the field, I was starting to get a bit of structure back to my life.

The mood swings weren't as frequent, and I suppose the endorphins that you get from exercise were positive. All of that was helping hugely.

Did I want to get back in with Kilkenny?

Absolutely, as I felt I had a point to prove... but mostly to myself. I'd won All Stars in 2010 and '11, had a so-so year in '12, but had a very poor year in '13, so my form was firmly on a downward trajectory.

There was the odd decent performance with the club and the county, but consistency was a big problem and probably coincided with the worst of the off-field issues I was facing. But in saying that, during our four in-a-row run, All Stars and all, I was in the middle of my addiction. Maybe not to the extent of where it was at when I hit rock bottom, but it was... always there, lurking in the background.

I'M IN A good place now.

I'm still going to my meetings every week and I'm doing the right things – and that's where I got to in the spring of 2014. Don't get me wrong, it was never going to be a case where I could turn around and say, 'I'm cured'... or... 'I'm never going to have a bet again' and that it was all in the past.

That's not the way it works.

In counselling, you look at other aspects of your life as well, not just the hurling and not just work. You look at relationships, you look at... well, everything, and you try to find the triggers that cause you to go on these binges or to have these slips. And, you know, I suppose that was probably a journey in itself.

This was something I'd never done before; I'd never had counselling or anything as in-depth as that because I'd felt there was no reason to do it previously.

It's amazing to say this, but my 2014 fitness levels were probably the best that they'd ever been... and I'd been on the Kilkenny senior panel since 2005. I was never a big fan of the pre-season training. I always struggled with the running and especially the endurance stuff.

Like, I'd do the runs all day... up and down the field. It's not as if we were running five or 10 kilometres or anything like that... you were talking about 200, 300, 400-metre runs... take a break... and go again. I just hated them.

The shorter spurts... of 30, 40 and 50 metres, they were probably the way I hurled as well; the sharp sprints, taking your man on and stuff like that. The work I did with Mickey was top class.

IN EARLY APRIL, I was brought back into training. Derek told me he had spoken to Brian; they were doing fitness tests in Carlow IT at the time, so off I went.

I didn't play towards the latter stages of the league but featured in the final against Tipp. I don't know if Brian or anyone in the management team had said anything to the players or the panel with regards to me being missing. I still don't know. I never asked the question and none of the lads did either. Eoin Murphy is a first cousin of mine and he was in the panel by then. I would have been in contact with him but the question wasn't asked. And do you know what? That may have been for the best in the long run.

When I came back in, there weren't any arched eyebrows or whispers in the corner of the dressing-room about me *swanning* back in. They all would have known that I was training like a dog with Mickey. I don't know if they knew that I was meeting Derek as well, and I still I don't know. But none of that really bothered me at the time.

I suppose my concentration was on the fitness tests and trying to improve every fitness test that I did. I think I did three or four with them, and the aim was to improve each time, which I did. And maybe then, they might have seen the hard work that I'd been doing.

'You'll be back in for training on Friday night' Derek said to me one night… and that was it. It was kind of surreal in a way, but I was back.

I could also sense that I was moving into a better place.

Maybe Brian had weighed things up and reckoned that if I'd got my house in order off the field, that I had a role to play again for him and that I did have something to offer. I felt that I did. There was no sit-down meeting or anything like that.

I was back in, and as much a part of the panel as anyone else.

WINNING THE LEAGUE against Tipp after extra time was a great way to restart my inter-county year and from there, it was all about pushing on. I started against Galway in the championship on a real hot June day in Tullamore. An incident happened in the second-half where I came in front of my man and our legs collided… I smashed my knee off the ground and it was like hitting concrete.

I went to get up and I went to go back into my position and the leg just went from underneath me… the knee just wobbled. I didn't know what was going on.

Eventually, I had to come off.

I'd injured my posterior cruciate, the PCL, the one at the back of the knee and I was thinking to myself, *Christ I must be cursed*. I'd got myself back into good shape physically; mentally I was I was in a good place and, then, I was hit with an injury that I didn't know how long it might end up keeping me out. I didn't know whether I was going to need an operation or not.

It's something you don't necessarily need an operation for so I opted to build the muscles around the knee as support and then heavily strap the knee for when I did get back – which was the All-Ireland semi-final against Limerick.

I came on with about maybe 20 minutes to go in what was a monsoon that particular day at Croke Park. The big debate was over myself and Eoin Larkin, and which one of us got the goal; a picture I got a few months later proved it hit off my hurl. Larks had been claiming it up until that point, but I remember putting the picture up in our WhatsApp group and we had a bit of craic over that.

I felt good coming into the Limerick game because I knew I had the work done in what was, largely, my own pre-season. As part of my rehab, I'd been in The Watershed swimming complex doing aqua jogging with Mick Dempsey, and I did a lot of spinning sessions. I worked really hard on maintaining my fitness and, most importantly of all, I was fresh, I was hungry... I was just mad for hurling having missed out on so much with the club and with Kilkenny.

I then had a clear four-week run then at the final against Tipp, though we would have hurled a game at Carrickshock the week after the Limerick game. That's the way our championship at the time was played. So that gave me another game under my belt and I got ready for the All-Ireland.

Now I didn't know whether I'd be starting or not, but I trained really well and then Brian picked me for the final in what ultimately turned into the two biggest games of 2014. On that first day, luckily enough for us, Hawkeye had been introduced. I'm still convinced to this day, if there was no Hawkeye, that that Bubbles Dwyer free would have been awarded – and given the way the supporters and Bubbles himself reacted, I think the umpire would have gone for the white flag. Thankfully, technology intervened.

I was very close to Bubbles when he hit the free, but I didn't actually even look at it. I remember turning and I looked up at Hill 16, didn't even look at him striking the ball... didn't look at it going over the post or over the bar or wherever it went.

I remember then, just looking up to the big screen to the left, where the old Nally Stand used to be, which told us that a Hawkeye decision was coming up.

The sign went red for 'Nil'... I drew a deep breath and said, *Thank God* to myself. The final whistle went from the resulting puck-out, so we knew we'd have to do it all over again. Kilkenny 3-22 Tipperary 1-28, and I got two of our goals.

I remember leaving Croke Park that day, thinking we'd been lucky and unlucky.

We put ourselves in a position to win the game though then we could just as easily have lost it at the end, but the bottom line was that we were still in the championship and we still had a savage chance. The window between then and the replay gave me an opportunity to put the head down again. The feeling within the panel was clear... we wanted to right a lot of wrongs from the drawn match.

The backs weren't happy with how the game went because the scoring was just astronomical, and for our backs, a repeat of the first day's high scoring just wasn't a runner for them.

It just couldn't happen again.

AND IT DIDN'T.

I got my hands on Liam MacCarthy again.

My most satisfying and unlikeliest Celtic Cross given everything that had gone on over the previous 11 months, with all those plates spinning. But I'd kept them spinning.

I'd found a way to climb the mountain again, especially during that spell between the Galway and Limerick matches when I couldn't train. That was a golden opportunity for the imp on my shoulder to whisper something in my ear and for me to do a handbrake turn at the worst possible moment, and head back onto a road I'd needed to remain well clear of.

Did I think about gambling?

Absolutely.

Was the temptation there?

Absolutely. Because during those times when I gave into the whispering imp, off I went and had the few bets. I knew dad, mam and the lads would have been worried around that time about the potential hammer blow that'd undo all the good work I'd put in over the previous six months or so. Only this time, I didn't listen to the imp.

I stayed the course. My counselling in Dublin, my GA meetings and focusing on doing the right things, all that took on a huge level of significance for me.

The biggest thing of all that occurred to me around this time was the fact that I'd emerged from the fog, even though I was only at the outset of my recovery. The numbness was gone. I could feel things emotionally again.

I hadn't felt that in the fog.

I'd not felt much at all when I was running on fumes. When I wasn't sleeping. When my diet was all over the place. When I wasn't doing the right things off the field to help my mind and my body to rest and recover.

I was like a ship with no rudder.

RECOVERY LAYS OUT the path to doing things head on rather than push them to the back of your mind. Recovery gives you back your emotions.

You start feeling things for what they actually are, rather than pretending you're fine, or just going through the motions… because that's how I was through quite a few of the All-Ireland wins. I'd had a lot more going on and weighing me down than I realised… until I asked for help.

LOOKING BACK ON 2014, the journey to get back into the panel and then the starting team, gives me the greatest sense of pride. My parents and family knew what I'd gone through as well and what we as a family had gone through. They would have seen how things were spiralling for me away from hurling, off the field.

It was very hard on them as well. I'd proven to myself that I could get back into the team. I've never doubted my ability as a hurler. That's not in any way being arrogant or cocky. I always backed myself when it came to the skills of the game.

But I suppose, the thing I always needed to work on was my fitness. So, applying myself then to gym work and recovery work took on a whole new meaning for me during recovery – just as life in general did.

When you're engulfed in addiction, you just don't see things with any sort of clarity. To emerge from that fog and win another All-Ireland, with both John and myself scoring goals, and to really appreciate and soak up every moment of that day, will always be incredibly special to me.

★★★

ENDA McEVOY

WITH ABOUT EIGHT minutes left in the 2014 All-Ireland final, Richie goes down the right wing, and his brother John was inside him. If Richie taps it over the bar, Kilkenny would have been five points clear.

But he throws it inside to the brother… the ball is lost, Tipp come down the field and reduce their arrears to three points – so there was a two-point swing in double quick time. And it's not necessarily because of a poor decision by Richie… he was always looking to put the ball into a better position for a score as opposed to concentrating on his own stats.

Go back to the drawn match against Tipp that year, that first goal Richie scored, when he flicked the ball beyond Darren Gleeson and tapped it into the net... it was astonishing. There's never been a goal scored like that in an All-Ireland final.

And for his second goal, he was going to shoot off his hurley, then he stopped... took it into his hand and then struck a brilliant goal. Minutes before that, Richie had put over a superb point from wide on the right side of the field. It was an outstanding performance in one of the great All-Ireland finals.

And come the replay, from a Michael Fennelly sideline, he pulled down the ball, he held off Kieran Bergin and bounced the ball into the bottom corner. Richie was THE man in those two All-Ireland finals. Just brilliant stuff.

Just imagine if Richie hadn't had to retire from inter-county hurling and he played on for another five years with Kilkenny, taking him up to 33?

Just imagine him and TJ Reid together?

Just imagine the heat Richie would have taken off TJ?

Just imagine.

★★★

RICHIE SNR

AFTER EVERYTHING CAME out, I know I was a lot more alert and tuned into the extent of the problem – and we don't mind talking about it now.

Once we got over that Friday night, you could see light at the end of the tunnel. We knew what we had to do, and we went and did it. I rang Oisín McConville, who I'd have met on a couple of occasions previously, including All Star trips.

I was coming out by the Woodford Dolmen Hotel in Carlow when I rang him and I ended up on the phone with him all the way back to Kilkenny, and I said I had no problem going up to meet him. I said we'd go up the following Saturday morning and we met Oisín at the Carrickdale Hotel.

We'd a three-hour conversation, which proved a massive help in getting over this problem and helping us to move on.

Oisín was absolutely brilliant; talking about how bad this could get if we didn't nip it in the bud, as he knew well himself, given where he'd come from. Coming down in the car, I was throwing out a few questions to Richie and we spoke about how low this problem can go and how big a problem this is.

But thank God, Richie is now in a great position; he did the podcast with Oisín and Thomas Niblock on the BBC and that was part of his process of coming to terms with it all and it was very well received. For me, my own eyes are now open to the problem in a way they never were prior to Richie admitting that he had an issue.

At the time, I was covering three counties in the job I was in… and the amount of people I'd been dealing with for years who came up to me and said they admired Richie for putting his hand up and talking about it, well that was all very reassuring.

Doing that stopped most of the whispering, I felt.

Back in the spring, I got a phone call from a guy that I'd dealt with on the road for 30 years and he was telling me about an employee he'd had on the books for 16 years, whom he trusted completely and it turned out that he'd a gambling problem. I asked Richie to meet him and he was absolutely brilliant with him.

The lad's boss rang me afterwards and said he felt they had him back in the right direction. That boss could have just as easily gone the other way, thrown the kitchen sink at him and rang the Gardaí.

But he didn't and I really admire the way he handled it.

Gambling is a significant problem and it could be any family's problem. I know there are people out there with drink problems, there are people out there smoking God knows what, but gambling is a serious, *serious* problem in this country. One bad day could mean you lose everything… your house, your relationship, your job… and it could all happen, sat in your sitting room, between your phone and the television.

The whole lot, lost in a matter of hours.

Alcoholism can, for some, be death by a thousand cuts but, of course, there's no hierarchy when it comes to addiction.

When you're rearing kids, you're doing it with the knowledge that some obstacle or mishap could be just around the corner. And maybe we were going around with our heads in the sand regarding Richie and the gambling problem, but look, at least we got to it before it was too serious.

It's behind us now and you just have to move on with life.

This problem can land on anyone's doorstep and people should realise that, and be aware of that. Once everything came out on the table that night, in the kitchen… your head, for those first few minutes, is probably in a funny place, but we just moved on from it then. That evening in the kitchen was ground zero… and has every day after that been a better one?

One hundred percent.

We were keeping an eye on things and as a family we stuck together. Richie was never the black sheep because of it, not at any stage. We realised that this was a problem that didn't have to remain a problem and that if we worked together, we'd get it sorted.

And thank God we did just that.

★★★

ANN

RICHIE'S ISSUE WASN'T unique to him.

We've read and heard about other stories in the past few years and it's something quite a few families have had to face, and I'd say there are a lot more who've had to deal with it and are still dealing with it now.

It's one of these things that can grow and grow.

But look, it's been solved now in as much as it can be and, hopefully, it'll stay that way. Richie has put huge time and commitment into managing the club and he's definitely got a lot out of it – and it's not straightforward either when he's managing two of his brothers. But the three of them have got on well with each other that way too, and that's a good reflection on all of them.

★★★

JAMIE

THERE'S A DEFINITE difference in Richie now compared to 10 years ago when things came to a head. But it's always going to be there and it's always going to be a worry. That's the reality of addiction.

Gambling isn't readily visible the way some addictions are, which makes it harder to detect early on – and sadly for some people, when the wider word gets out there, it's too late for them. But thankfully, Richie is in a good place now and has been for quite some time. Gambling is in his past, and family is family; we rowed right in behind Richie and supported him. He has two lovely kids, a good relationship, a good job and please God, there'll be lots more good times ahead for all of them.

★★★

STEPHANIE

WHEN THE PODCAST with Thomas Niblock was about to drop, that did come as a bit of a surprise to us, alright. But it was certainly a good thing for Richie to do.

As a family, out of respect for Richie, we never spoke about it publicly but we supported him before and after it became headline news. I was a guard for four years and I did two weeks in Cork as a student in Tabor Lodge, where I spoke to people with eating disorders, along with alcoholics, drug addicts and gambling addicts.

Sitting in on some of their meetings and seeing what they were going through left a huge impression me, so when Richie's issue came to light, I knew there wasn't an easy road ahead of him.

But thankfully, he has come out the other side of it and just got on with living. It's great to see him in a better place and putting that work ethic into himself, first and foremost.

★★★

SUZANNE

I WAS QUITE young when Richard's off-field problem became known and I was shielded from a good bit of it initially, even though people knew and we had a sense that something wasn't quite right.

I was sat down once or twice to be told a few bits, but when you're young, you pick up on the sense of something not being right with someone at home – and I heard bits and pieces from other rooms, thinking back on it now. But I can't imagine what Richard *was feeling at the time and the level of pressure that he was under.*

He was playing and training at pretty much a professional level, he was working and he had a young child… and then all of that was going on behind the scenes. But he has changed his whole world around and he's in a better place now.

Life has changed for the better and hurling remains such an important part of Richard's life.

Sure, we all just want the best for each other and it's great to see things going so well for him.

★★★

RICHIE JNR

I'LL ALWAYS HAVE savage regrets when it comes to my inter-county career; some players will say they've none and that they 'left it all on the line' and so on.

But can I say that? Probably not.

And would I change things if I could go back?

One hundred percent… and it's something I've mentioned at more than one GA meeting. What impacted me off the field is the thing I'd undo, if I could step into a time machine.

Could I have dealt with the problem earlier than I did, rather than leaving it fester and become an even bigger problem for both myself and those closest to me?

And did I always give 100 percent to recovery and things away from the training field? No, I didn't and there's no point in me suggesting otherwise.

Did I reach my full potential at inter-county level?

HERE'S THE THING.

From the outside, looking in, most people would say that I probably did.

Personally, I don't think I did, even though there were certain heights that I reached. And look, eight All-Irelands in 11 years is pretty good going.

But from a performance point of view, giving to the team and adding to the all-round effort, I probably could have given more if I'd been at my peak off the field. I probably didn't stand out and produce the sort of play that'd end up on *The*

Sunday Game analysis reel.

But when the fog cleared, and I began to manage life better away from hurling, that's what made 2014 and '15 with Kilkenny so memorable, even though the knee injury was curtailing me somewhat by then. And to end up winning an All-Ireland with the club and my brothers in 2017 and really contributing to that, that's always going to be a huge highlight for me, both in hurling and personal terms.

But was I the most committed, was I very committed or was I even 50 percent committed to it? At times I wasn't.

We've all read books and heard stories of other players that have struggled with their own issues, such as Oisín McConville, for example. I don't think people realise just how much an addiction can impact on everything and everybody around you, unless they actually experience it for themselves.

In my own family, we'd never had anything like this to try and deal with. There was one night that Jamie was sat in the kitchen with tears in his eyes because he could see what it was doing to me, but also what I was doing to them.

And I don't think I'd thought about that up until I hit rock bottom.

I never thought about what I was doing to them. The whole county and probably the whole country had an idea that I had a problem, but it was never publicised. I know for a fact it would have been said to dad, because dad would have worked in the pub trade and it would have been said to him because he was going in and out of pubs... and I suppose that's where a lot of people going in and out of the bookies would have seen me or would have spoken to me.

I know it was said to him.

It was the same for Jamie on nights out; he doesn't drink so he would have had lads coming up to him saying, 'If only your brother would spend as much time on the hurling field as he does in the bookmakers' and stuff like that.

This was constantly happening to Jamie.

He wasn't too sure how to deal with, and sure I suppose I wasn't either.

SINCE 2014, BOTH on and off the field, I've been able to feel things in a fuller, more emotional way than I ever could in the years previous when gambling just swamped everything. I really embraced the build-up to the 2014 All-Ireland final and, in certain respects, enjoyed it. There was no fog interrupting my view that year... the way I could remember captaining Kilkenny and scoring the winning point when we won the minor All-Ireland in 2003, beating Galway by 2-16 to 2-15.

2015 wasn't quite as enjoyable for me due to the injury but I could still appreciate us winning the All-Ireland in a fuller way than I had previously. But the cherry on top was still ahead of me. Winning the All-Ireland with the club in 2017 was something I could only dream of prior to that.

The ultimate dream, of course, was a senior championship and then a senior All-Ireland but for a small parish like Carrickshock, that intermediate All-Ireland will forever stand out in the club's history. The senior dream is still there, but that's for another group of players to fulfil now.

To have the butterflies before that final in Croke Park and then to be out on that field with my two brothers, surrounded by lads you've known your whole life… with my family up in the stand… and to be able to genuinely be in the moment, it was pure magic.

There was no shitshow in the background.

I was completely swept up in the satisfaction of being part of something really special. To go to Croke Park with Carrickshock for an All-Ireland final was an *amazing* feeling. To win an All-Ireland there with the club was just off the charts.

It really was the happy ending to a long and winding road.

Sure, there'd been lots of bumps along the way to get there, but I could never have imagined a better end to my playing days. To be able to fully enjoy it, and be swept up in the pure emotion of that All-Ireland win was one of the greatest experiences of my life.

LIFE LESSONS COME at all of us in different ways. Undoing the problems gambling led to has been my biggest life challenge, but I can't let that define me.

That's the greatest single challenge in recovery: to not let what went before define who you become during recovery and all the years that'll follow that. For most of my life, I had a tendency to look back and I only started to undo that habit until two years ago… and that's years into recovery.

I was living in the past, whereas I should have been looking forward.

And I was looking back on absolutely everything, thinking about the people that my addiction affected, the person that I was during my addiction… which I don't look back on fondly. Was I being true to myself?

I know now that I wasn't. You're just so numb inside when you're dealing with an addiction, that feelings don't really come to the surface because you're blocking them all. You just don't feel the regular things you ought to feel in a life without addiction. So, there was a major, negative impact on relationships that I would have had, and with family and friends. I lost friends because of it, and lost contact with people that I'd have been very close to, because you isolate yourself from everyone when you're in addiction. It's a vicious circle and I spent years looking back, pretty much lost in the past and wondering how and when I'd move on from all those thoughts... to reaching the point where I'd deal with it, get counselling, get to meetings and reach a point where I could park things. Pull up that handbrake and then know when I'd release it again. That I'd be moving forward, and stop dwelling on what I'd done in the past.

And then I asked for help. The fog began to clear.

I stopped letting my past define me and that's been the single biggest thing I've learned in recovery. That's helped me become a better person. That's helped me to be true to myself and those closest to me, and to starting looking forward to a future with my sons, with my relationship, with my family, all the while conscious of trying to be a better person than I had been in the middle of addiction.

I'LL BE A compulsive gambler until the day I die – and I'll go to my meetings every week, and I'll do that for the rest of my life. That's all part of recovery.

Some people might think that if you go five, 10, 15, 20 years free of a bet, that somehow, you're cured and that if you've gone years without a bet that you don't need to go to your meetings. To me, that's not how it works.

I've rationalised it by considering myself sick and that the meetings are my medicine, so in essence it's no different to someone who needs to top up on medication. I realise that might sound odd to some people, but I don't, because I don't ever want to go back to where I was and the madness of my life when I was actively gambling.

I wouldn't wish it on anyone. In order for me not to ever go back there, I attend my meetings... that's my medicine. At the meetings, I hear the war stories, so to speak; have a cup of tea with lads that have gone through the same and a lot worse than I have, and the bond you build through those conversations is amazing.

The world is so small when you're in the grip of addiction, with bombs going off that only you, the addict, can hear exploding – and then you're at the meetings and you hear other war stories and you realise, *It's not just me that's been going through all of this.* And that's part of recovery.

I KNOW THAT I can't rewind the clock.

I've accepted that it's part of who I am, it's part of a past that I cannot change. But it's time to move on.

And life now is about building a future without any of that, and trying to right the wrongs by making it up to those who were impacted most during my years in the fog.

V

The Black
and Amber

★★★

★★★

RICHIE JNR

WHEN I GOT the phone call in December 2004 to come onto the senior panel, it's obviously a phone call that you're hoping to get. And then when the call came through, the excitement was huge.

You're brought in on a certain date, you're brought through a gym program, your fitness levels are tested, training begins… and everything just took off from there. Was there ever a time that I kind of felt, *Jesus, I'm out of my depth here?*

I don't think there was, but obviously at the start when you're going into a dressing-room and DJ Carey and Henry Shefflin are sitting there… and then you see Peter Barry and Noel Hickey across from you, I did think, initially, *F**k, do I have a right to be here?*

Do I have to prove that I belong here and that I deserve this?

But that actually drove me on from the very beginning. And that's not to say you lose that drive because I knew, even though I was very lucky to be a starter from probably the word 'go' and all the way for most of my career… I knew that a drop in form, standards and performances had a consequence when you had, at different times, the likes of Taggy Fogarty, Eddie Brennan, TJ Reid and Richie Hogan sitting on the bench… waiting for their moment… ready to go whenever the opportunity arose.

That was in the back of my mind every day when I went out.

I knew I had to not only maintain the same standards, I had to raise the bar. That's what wearing the Kilkenny jersey demands of you as a player.

★★★

RICHIE SNR

I HAD THE honour of being the first Carrickshock player from the actual parish to tog out with the Kilkenny senior hurlers, and that means lot to me. I was a sub in the under-21 panel in 1977, then I played in an under-21 Leinster final on a Wednesday night in 1978 and the following morning, when I was piking bales at home with my father, Ned, the Lord have mercy on him, we heard the sound of the local postman's Honda 50 coming towards us.

He came around the corner and told m,: 'Richie, you're to be in Kilkenny tomorrow night for training'.

That's how I found out.

I nearly fell off the trailer of bales with the shock of it. The nearest phone to us in those days was in the post office in Hugginstown… and the message was then relayed from the post office via the Honda 50.

THOSE FIRST FEW nights of training went well for me, but we lost the Leinster senior final to Wexford by three points (3-17 to 3-14) in what was Eddie Keher's last championship appearance for Kilkenny. It also marked the end of the road for Pat Delaney with the county due to a knee injury. Then, as I told Enda McEvoy in a *Sunday Independent* interview in May 1990:

'I faded off the (Kilkenny) scene completely. Four years later I was lucky – Carrickshock were doing well at the time, Glenmore beat us in the intermediate semifinal after a replay, and that helped bring me to the attention of the (inter-county) selectors.'

Following on from our county junior title in 1979, two years later we pushed a really strong Glenmore team – featuring Christy Heffernan, Willie O'Connor and 'Titch' Whelan – all the way, but they got past us after a replay (5-11 to 3-7) and went on to win the intermediate crown at what was the start of their great era.

I was coming off the field that day when Mick O'Neill, the chairman of the Kilkenny County Board called out for me, then came over to me and asked, 'Will you tog out with the Kilkenny panel tomorrow?' Of course, I said yes. I was told the time I was to meet the panel the following day, and when I came home that evening, all the Carrickshock lads were all heading out for pints as most teams do at the end of the year.

I'd a match the following day to take into account, so I had two bottles of Club Orange and quietly made my exit just as the craic was starting. I got home, went to bed early, was up and out to Mass the following morning (Sunday, October 3)… then off to Nowlan Park for myself.

The team was named and, to my total surprise, I got the nod to start at centre-forward, the first time I started for the Kilkenny seniors who were in Division 1B of the National League at the time. I was only after playing a match the previous day, so I was completely gobsmacked to have got the nod.

In hindsight, slipping off home after two oranges was one of the best decisions I'd ever made up to that point. We won by 1-19 to 1-9, which was an improvement on the following year's headline making draw in Killarney. The *Kilkenny People* match report suggested we didn't exactly set the world on fire that cold afternoon:

'The game was totally lacking in atmosphere and the home players didn't appear to have a great appetite for the match. Indeed, had the Northern junior hurling final not been the curtain-raiser, then the attendance would have been very sparse… Overall it was a poor opening to the League for Kilkenny, who have set promotion as their top priority. It is hard to pick out anyone as doing particularly well, but the best hurling was turned in by Ger Fennelly, Maurice Mason (and) late in the match, Richard Power and Kieran Brennan.'

WE MIGHT NOT have been too hot that day but still, it was nice to get some kind of a nod in the paper the following week. Pat Henderson, who had been involved in the Kilkenny selectors' group the year before, came in as manager and the hope was that we'd improve and get back into contention again.

But I don't think anyone in the county that autumn could have foreseen us winning successive Leinster, All-Ireland and National League titles in the two years that followed.

As chairman, Mick O'Neill would have had a big say when it came to selecting the team at that time. A Kilmacow man, Mick was a tremendous chairman and I'll be forever grateful that he showed faith in me. With the county in Division 1B in 1981, there was an undeniable sense that we were in a bit of a lull, and it's during those fallow periods that selectors cast the net that little bit wider than you might do during the more successful spells.

The good times definitely make it tougher on a really good player in, say, Slieverue, Kilmacow, Piltown, or even our own club, to make a dent in a county panel, even though we were spoiled during the golden era under Brian Cody in terms of representation. Lads coming from small clubs need to be given every encouragement that they can get, to keep believing they can make the grade.

Take a club such as Piltown… the last player they had in the Kilkenny senior panel was Liam McCarthy 30-plus years ago. I love seeing players from outside the 'establishment' clubs in Kilkenny making it into the senior inter-county panel. It's pretty easy to be successful in a big club; it's harder to get lads to keep it going in clubs that are struggling.

It's something the GAA shouldn't take an eye off.

I remember us winning a league match in Casement Park against Antrim and I was throwing my gear into the bus afterwards when the late Pat Delaney, one of our selectors, gestured my way to head off down the street with him. Now Pat would have been to Casement Park previously and he knew exactly where he was going.

So we went into a pub, got a table and had a drink and he says to me, 'Richie, I'm telling you this… the jersey is yours and it's up to you to mind it'. Those words, coming from Pat, telling me I was good enough, was a huge confidence booster and you remember words like that. It's why it's so important, whatever walk of life you're in, to give a younger person you're sharing an office, a farm or a dressing-room with, an encouraging word.

The right words will stay with you for a lifetime, and after Pat's chat with me, I drove on from there.

I had fierce admiration for Pat as a hurler. For someone of his stature to say something like that to me meant a lot. I went on and played well in the league semi-final and final in 1982, and had a good year in the '82 championship. After that year, I really felt part of the whole set-up; I felt good enough to be there.

Of course, I had doubts when I was first called in about whether I'd be good enough to establish myself with this squad but, as it turned out, I ended up having 12 or 13 unbelievable years with the county.

After I first got into the Kilkenny panel, when training changed, I'd have felt tired a couple of times starting those early matches. I remember Jim Langton, the Lord of mercy on him, saying to me inside in Langton's when I was having my dinner, 'Richie, I'm going to give you one piece of advice… if you're tired going training, you shouldn't be going training. The body is telling you that you need rest.'

Those were words that I've never, ever forgotten. Rest, as is now well established, is an integral part of any well-considered training plan. You've other things you need to factor in: you're either studying or holding down a job while training hard with Kilkenny, and then you're trying to show your face in the field with your club as well.

That's a lot of balls to keep juggling for months at a time.

PLAYING IN THE half-forward line with Kilkenny, my main job was to contest everything, be it in the air or on the ground. Overhead striking was big in the game and you were always encouraged to do what you could in terms of feeding the inside line. And if it came low to you at an angle, instead of maybe going out to pick it up, we had to get that ball into the full-forwards. Billy Fitz and Liam Fennelly were the two great forwards of our team. They were real finishers and got some brilliant scores for Kilkenny over the years.

Another of our jobs was to stop the opposition half-back line from dominating and that was a repeated pre-match instruction. We knew most of Noel Shekan's puck-outs were going to land down on top of us, so we had to be on our toes at all times.

In the 1982 All-Ireland final against Cork, I was on Dermot MacCurtain and 20 minutes in, I'd had very little impact on the game. Then Noel Skehan pucked this ball down my direction, which I caught with my left hand – I'd normally come back to my right – and put it over the bar from about 40 yards, which was a fierce relief for me. The few balls that had previously come my way up until then had been swept up by MacCurtain so that really got the blood pumping.

I'd scored in an All-Ireland final for the first time… and three further points from play followed that day. It gave me huge confidence.

Kieran Brennan and myself wore 10 and 12 for quite a few years; we moved the ball on the ground and through the air. We were contesting everything, anticipating every puck-out and you just had to be manning yourself up. It was a more instinctive game and, I feel, more enjoyable to be playing that way rather than the current trend to go short so much of the time. Now the emphasis is all on 'the process'. Players are as afraid to step outside the game plan as they are to give interviews. And I don't know if it's good for the game.

The weekend that I played in my first All-Ireland senior semi-final against Galway in 1982, I didn't know how serious things were with our baby daughter, Celine Mary. Coming home that evening on the train to Cork, I felt I was really after contributing... a forward from a small junior club having scored 1-3 from play to help Kilkenny into the final.

But, of course, the night unfolded in the saddest terms possible for Ann and myself when it came to Celine, the Lord have mercy on her. Celine was born the Tuesday after the semi-final and then we buried her.

To say that was a really tough week is an understatement.

★★★

ANN

LIFE, AS IS the case for everyone, has had its ups and downs. We lost our third child, Celine Mary, before the 1982 All-Ireland semi-final but I didn't tell Richie until after the game had been played that Sunday.

I'd known since the Saturday night, when I went into St Finbarr's Hospital and was told that she wasn't going to make it. We were after doing the shopping, when I said to Richie that I hadn't been feeling what I ought to have been feeling at that stage of my pregnancy; so we went into hospital to get things checked. It was a sensation I hadn't felt when carrying Jamie or Stephanie. I was at full-term at the time.

So in I went, and they sat me down and told me they couldn't find the baby's heartbeat... they could only detect mine. So they told me there and then.

They then left it up to me as to when I told Richie the sad news.

I really felt it wasn't in his best interests to tell him the news right then, what with him playing Galway in an All-Ireland semi-final the next day. Something that was beyond our control had happened and all the crossed fingers in the world couldn't undo what had happened. He had the biggest match of his life the following day and I wanted it to go well for him.

I knew how much that match meant to Richie, and I wanted him to succeed every ounce as much as he did himself. So I made the decision not to tell him until he came back from Dublin. And, of course, it was hard not to tell him.

So Richie travelled up from Cork on the train.

If I'd told him beforehand, he wouldn't have gone to Croke Park. And then the day of the match I went out to a friend's house in Carrigtwohill. Celine was born the following Tuesday.

When I told Richie, he broke down and asked why I hadn't told him.

Even Paddy Grace, the Kilkenny County Board chairman said the same, and said they'd have flown Richie back to Cork from Dublin had they known. I suppose I was trying to be pragmatic about the situation there and then.

In my own head, I was telling myself… But sure what else could I do? Nothing was going to change to make this situation any better.

I'd a fairly straightforward theory at the time: I had to get up and get on with things or else I'd lie down and lie under it. I had to get up and keep going.

It was a very sad time but I feel it would have been worse if Celine had been our first.

When I'd had Stephanie in Cork, a woman from Midleton had a stillbirth and lo and behold would you believe it, the following year, when I had my stillbirth, that same woman had a little girl. Our roles had been reversed.

We had our time with Celine on our own, and then we brought Jamie and Stephanie in, which was a very special moment, having us all together for that short time. Richie and Tom Whelan brought Celine to Kilkenny for burial on the Friday

RICHIE SNR

A MONTH LATER in the All-Ireland final, I grew into the game and felt I contributed well, finishing up with four points from play and, looking back, those back-to-back performances probably made my inter-county career.

Those two matches will always stand out for me.

The *Kilkenny People* assessed my performance in pen-picture format:

'Looking at him on Sunday you would never know he was an intermediate player. He was deadly accurate with his shooting, with both right and left hand. Two points in succession in the second half knocked Cork back after they had just scored a goal. His

long-range point scoring was typical of the Kilkenny style. This was his first all-Ireland and he could hardly have expected to do any better.'

The night in Langton's that followed that win will never be forgotten. Two lads from the parish came up to me and told me I was needed in Delaney's on Patrick Street, which was Carrickshock's watering hole in Kilkenny.

When I went into the lounge that night, they just lifted me up.

It was phenomenal, seeing so many familiar faces who meant so much to me, who knew what Ann and I had been through. So much had happened in the previous month.

The emotions couldn't have been more separate from each other, to have lost Celine and then, a few weeks later, to win an All-Ireland medal. From there, we moved on in life and thank God we have five great kids and, in the greater scheme of things, sure we never had any real trouble.

And that's something to be able to say at this stage in our lives.

★★★

NICKY BRENNAN

TO WIN THE double-double was a significant achievement by any county and I know subsequent Kilkenny and Limerick teams have blown what we did out of the water in the meantime, but at that time, it was a rare occurrence in hurling terms and sure we were thrilled to make such progress so quickly.

We won well in '82 against the odds when we beat Cork, with Richie contributing four points from play. But the following year's final was a much tighter affair and Cork really came for revenge.

They won the toss and decided to play against the elements. By half-time, that looked like a good decision as we were only six points ahead (1-10 to 0-7) but we started the second-half in whirlwind fashion, with Richie scoring a goal a minute after the restart… and it really was a game changer.

A brace of Cork goals from Seanie O'Leary and Tómas Mulcahy made for a tight finish, but we managed to keep our heads in front.

★★★

ENDA McEVOY

RICHIE SNR'S FOUR points from play in the '82 All-Ireland final may not seem too hot in the context of what Limerick are currently producing but back then, you're talking about a slower game, a heavier ball and heavier pitches, so it was much harder.

Yet Richie, who wasn't hurling at senior level with his club, struck over four points in an All-Ireland senior final from 50/60 yards. And the following year, Richie's goal in the final against Cork gave Kilkenny the comfort blanket they needed to secure back-to-back MacCarthy Cups.

And, of course, winning the 'double double' was a huge achievement at the time; the '82 double was the first time Kilkenny had won both titles since 1933.

Those two campaigns remain stand-out achievements from a Kilkenny perspective.

★★★

RICHIE SENIOR

ANN AND MYSELF lived in Cork for a couple of years at a time when we didn't have too much to our name. And I got great opportunities to hurl with several clubs in Cork. I was offered good jobs too, and all I had to do was to sign the transfer form. But I just couldn't bring myself to do it.

That I never left the club that gave me the opportunity to wear the county jersey is something I'm very proud of. Playing in Cork would have certainly made life easier for me – and Ann was great when it came to Jamie and Stephanie; she'd often have put down days without seeing me at all. But I've always been a Carrickshock man through and through.

At the time, we needed every bit of luck that we could get… I was working a full-time and a part-time job for a decent spell, but we decided not to go down that road. There's nowhere like home.

While we were in Cork, I struck up a relationship with a man called Tom Whelan and his wife, Tess. Tom and I worked together; he was like a brother and a father to me. We just clicked from day one. Now, the full-time job was in a factory in Little Island, called Swissco, which supplied ready-made meals. I used to be in for 6am, and would finish around 3pm.

Tom was the chef there at the time and he was also working part-time at Water Rock House, which is located between Carrigtwohill and Midleton… and I also worked part-time there in the bar. Tom and Tess were brilliant to both Ann and myself and we remained unbelievable friends long after we'd moved back to Kilkenny.

Unfortunately, Tom (who had been chairman of the Panel of Chefs Ireland) died suddenly in February 2020 and it was a massive shock to us at the time. He used to come down to us here regularly and we had great times together. I was in the Midlands Park Hotel in Portlaoise when I got the call that Tom had died; that call stands out in my mind as much as the day I first wore the Kilkenny jersey as an under-14 player. It was an awful shock.

Tom's death was so hard to take.

BUT LET ME rewind the clock the guts of 40 years or more.

There was a chap with a business based in Greystones, in Wicklow, called Southern Veal and he used to call to Tom at Swissco. He wanted Tom to take over the whole Munster region. Eventually, Tom sat down with me for a chat about it.

'If I decide to take on this position, Richie, will you come with me?' he asked.

I replied, 'Look, Tom, if you decide to go, then… I'll go with you'. So, we took the leap together and it was absolutely flying along. I was on the road and I loved it; I gave 43 years on the road selling. But then, one day, the owner of the business dropped dead – and he was only 53 years old. It was a huge shock at the time and neither of us knew where we stood when it came to our employment. Six months later, we were informed that Irish Veal was buying out the Munster region, so we had to find other work.

Tom set up his own business, and I went into HB Ice Cream on the South Douglas Road and once I was in that job, that was probably the time in my own mind where I was nearest to us staying in Cork altogether. Our manager was a man called Ken Hannaway; I got on really well with him and it was a great company to work for.

However, I was sitting at home one night in the second half of 1982 when

Tommy Hoyne, the Carrickshock club treasurer at the time, rang me. 'Richie, there's a job in the *Kilkenny People* that might interest you… Barry's Tea are looking for a rep in the South East region.'

'Send it onto me,' I told him, 'I'll see what I make of it.'

So, I got the paper, applied for the job and in October 1982, I got called for an interview in the Newpark Hotel in Kilkenny. We were only after winning the All-Ireland and I never once mentioned anything whatsoever about hurling, I just didn't want to go down that road. I wanted to be offered the job on the strength of my interview and nothing else.

Now we loved Cork and at that stage, and we were just starting to see a bit of light at the end of the tunnel, but only for Tommy Hoyne sending me that ad from the *Kilkenny People*, the chances are that Richie would have hurled for Cork as we were just beginning to settle down there by then.

After three interviews, I was offered the Barry's Tea job by the Sales Director and he gave me a week to think about it. We decided to make for home and it worked out really well. We had wonderful people involved in Carrickshock, who in their own way also helped me to make that decision… Jimmy Walsh and John Cassin, who are no longer with us, and who were both presidents of the club at the time, Paddy Joe Rohan, Liam Duggan, Sean Raggett, Tommy Hoyne, and so on… and they really appreciated the fact that I took the Barry's job, moved back home and remained committed to the club.

Barry's wanted me stationed in Carlow, but I was anxious, if I could at all, to live in the parish that Ann and myself were born and reared in. I was delighted to still be hurling with the club, to be living in the parish and knowing that the kids were going to grow up here. We rented for 12 to 18 months, then we bought a site and built the house in 1984. It was tough going at the time, there's no denying that.

When we moved in, we had four sticks under the sink and a ladder going upstairs, but everyone was happy. We loved Cork, I was getting on great in the job down there but the draw of home was strong. And I had great friends back home. Noel Maher and myself were really, really great friends and still are today. If Noel hurled bad or I hurled bad, we'd head straight home… we just wouldn't go out. That's the way it was. My four brothers were hurling at the time; the Raggetts, the Phelans and the Dwyers were hurling. Jim Ireland was there, and Jimmy Sheehan was coming on the scene... and they all loved the jersey.

TRAINING WAS A different beast in my time from what it is now. In the late 80s and early 90s we really only trained for the championship. Frank Cummins and myself did a lot of training in Cork on our own. And all we were doing was keeping the bodies right and keeping ourselves as fit as we could.

I would have done a lot of training on my own too. Maybe the fact that I was coming from a small club, I had to convince myself that I had to be 100 percent, but Frank and myself did a nice bit of training for the couple of years I was in Cork. Frank and myself soldiered well together. He was well established in the Kilkenny panel by the time I came on the scene, but he made great time for me right from the off. And in travelling up and down from Cork together, we struck up an even better relationship.

We were coming down to train for the '82 All-Ireland final and, in those days, there was no such thing as taxis or getting a lad to drive you to or from training. We came down in Frank's car and shared the driving.

This particular night, Frank, who was in the demolition business, was after having a long day and had been up since 5.30am... and there I was thinking I was getting up out of the bed early... at 5.50. We came to Kilkenny, we trained and then we went to Langton's and had a bite to eat. Then off we went... and what happened next is only known by a few people.

We ended up in a dike on the way back to Cork, because we both fell asleep.

We were very, *very* lucky. Looking back on it, you'd be wondering how that training night could be beneficial after such a long working day. I didn't get back home to my house until just before 1am, similar to Frank, who was living in Blarney. We were living on the Kinsale Road. The way things have moved on now at inter-county level, it's hard to credit the things we were asked to do in my time.

But it was made a great deal easier with Frank's company. We're still great friends and we've had some great times together. He went to school in Stoneyford, he still has some great friends here, and he loves coming back. Sure, it's always great to see him.

The extraordinary thing, again taking Cork into consideration, is that I won a minor, under-21 and three senior All-Ireland medals... all against Cork.

THERE WAS NO such thing as coming down two nights a week in January, February or March. You really only came back to Kilkenny when the league was finishing up, and we were getting ready for the championship.

And when I came back to live in Stoneyford, once St Stephens' Day came, I togged out and headed out into a 25-acre field below where I was living. Jimmy Sheehan, a fierce Carrickshock clubman owned it, and that was where my pre-season began. I'd have had a lot done before Pat Henderson would have called us in prior to the championships in 1981 and '82, but I was always keen on being in good enough shape before the call came in for training with the county.

For me, as the first Carrickshock man to make the senior panel, the honour of being involved was huge and I just wanted to give myself every chance and be the best possible version of myself in hurling terms. And I never minded that at all. To be honest, I enjoyed it.

Hurling is not an easy game, but it's a lot more manageable when you're physically fit and match ready. And I knew I had to be in good shape to give a good account of myself and, more importantly, to help the team out in the best way possible.

Our last league match used to be played on the first Sunday in December. But if you'd hurled in an All-Ireland final, you wouldn't really have trained with the county team… since September! But, when I used to jump that wall and do a few rounds of Jimmy Sheehan's field, I'd know how much fitness I was after losing, and how far I'd fallen back. But I always enjoyed it, which was obviously a huge help.

Speaking of huge helps, Ann is as involved in the GAA and loves it as much as any of us in the house. And her love of hurling was and remains one of the biggest and best supports I've had in my whole life. If there was someone in the house who had no interest in the GAA, I'd have faced a much different scenario over the past four or more decades.

Ann supported and encouraged me in the best way possible. If I was due to go training and if I was any way lazy about it, I used to be nearly pushed out the door to go training. That was the level of backing I had, which made my hurling career so much more manageable.

In hindsight, I can't ever thank Ann enough… for everything.

I had huge time for the likes of Pat Delaney and Kieran Purcell, who would have been a bit ahead of me in hurling terms, and Tommy Walsh… described by Michael O'Hehir as 'The blonde bombshell from Thomastown'.

Tommy lost an eye hurling against Tipperary in the 1967 All-Ireland final, which sadly brought a premature end to his career. He had looked set to reach another level with his hurling ability, his pace and his skill. What happened that day was a complete accident but it was a huge shame, nonetheless.

And I had massive respect for Paddy Grace, who was secretary of the Kilkenny County Board for so many years. He looked after players brilliantly and always commanded his brief, and the respect he got across every grade and from every club in the county was phenomenal. I was fortunate to be in the company of so many good administrators, given my initial step into that particular breach with Carrickshock while I was still hurling with the county.

IN 1986, GER Fennelly and myself were in midfield for Kilkenny. We'd a good league and a great Leinster Championship behind us by the time we met Galway in the All-Ireland semi-final; the year they played a third midfielder and blew us out the water in Thurles, winning by 4-13 to 0-12.

That had never been seen before at that level, and it really worked for them on the day. They went for it again in the All-Ireland final against Cork, but it didn't work out for them. That was a great era for Galway, reaching four successive finals from 1985 to '88, and winning three MacCarthy Cups in 1980, '87 – when they got the better of us – and in '88. From that team, I know Sylvie Linnane and Stevie Mahon very well, and I still meet them both once or twice a year.

We've all made great relationships years on from when we were mad to beat each other. In '86 they felt they had to do something a little different after we'd beaten them in that year's league final but they deserved their win in Semple. Just consider some of the names on that team: Conor Hayes, Sylvie, the sadly missed Tony Keady, Gerry McInerney, Pete Finnerty, Stevie, Pat Malone, Brendan Lynskey, Martin Naughton, Eanna Ryan… they were strong, they were fast, and they were skilful, and they deserved the success that came their way, even if some of it was at Kilkenny's expense… and that brings me to the 1987 All-Ireland final.

I don't like using the word 'bitterness' about pretty much anything but it springs to mind when I think about that final… I can't avoid it.

Galway were hell-bent on beating us during that era – and the feeling was mutual. I'm not 100 percent sure where the bit of edge between the two counties came from; I recall Cyril Farrell being interviewed by RTE around that time and somewhere along the way we ended up being labelled as a 'physical outfit' but, for me, everyone was physical, that's the way hurling was played at the time.

And Galway were as tough as any team that hurled in the 80s. As a spectacle, the '87 All-Ireland final was a poor enough game, but you don't tend to mind games being poor when you win them. But we lost that day, scoring only nine points, as Galway won scoring only 1-12. You wouldn't win an All-Ireland with that scoring nowadays but no one gets out of bed on the morning of a match like that, not wanting to perform.

But that's what happened that day for us, and Galway went home with the cup.

From time to time, there was talk about Galway only having a handful of matches to turn up for, when it came to the championship. The Connacht final, with the greatest of respect to Roscommon, was a foregone conclusion in the years that it was played. But, if anything, that placed Galway at a disadvantage, as they had to be on it right from the throw-in of an All-Ireland semi-final to have any chance of winning.

Coming in at the semi-final stage like that wasn't the answer for Galway, both for their players and their supporters. They hadn't any run of going through the summer and enjoying matches in, say, Thurles or Cusack Park, and must have found it difficult to build momentum ahead of a big match against whoever came out of Leinster or Munster.

They ended up having to get ready for one big match every year... and they'd no league campaign to get them match-ready, the way counties have nowadays. Where Galway is now in terms of the structures, at all the grades in Leinster, its giving their younger players better chances and more big match experience. You'd suspect that's going to make Galway a stronger and more consistent county in Liam MacCarthy terms over the next 10 to 15 years. And that can only be positive for the overall health of the game.

WHEN YOU WOKE up on a Monday morning after a championship match, if every bone in your body wasn't sore, there was something wrong.

There's a much higher level of fitness now, and better recovery, so a lot of that post-match soreness has been lessened and players are all the better because of that. However tough the matches were, I never once felt that an opposing player was sent out to stick me out over the sideline and leave me there.

However, there were a lot of Sunday matches that left you feeling like you'd been in a battle once you were out of bed the following morning.

At club level, Eddie and Willie O'Connor from Glenmore were as tough as they'd come and brilliant hurlers into the bargain. For men who weren't particularly big, they were outstanding competitors and never gave an inch. When I was a senior selector with Kilkenny in 1996 and '97, Willie delivered a template of what a player ought to do when training.

The work that he put into the drills and the warm-ups, before a game would start, would have the sweat rolling off him. He probably felt that he had to work that bit harder, because physically he wasn't a huge presence. Willie had some dedication to training! I'd say the fact that he knew himself, that physically he was going to be outmuscled maybe in one-to-one battles, that was why he worked so hard on every element of his hurling, including his first touch.

If you had 20 to 25 guys lads like Willie training, it'd be very hard to stop a group with that level of commitment. Both the O'Connors were great hurlers, and fine servants to Kilkenny.

I'd have had some good battles with Malachy Hogan and John Ryan of Dunnamaggin, Tommy Frisby of Mullinvat, and Bobby Jackman of Windgap, who is sadly not with us anymore.

Bobby was a tough bit of stuff. Bobby and I were marking each other in a relegation match, when both of us were injured – both having cracked ribs – but we knew it was a match we couldn't afford to sit out. Granted, I look back on it now and there's no way either of us should have been playing. I'd fierce time for Bobby, and we ended up being great friends.

Joe Hennessy probably had the best first touch of any hurler I ever played with. It was like there was glue on the bottom of his hurley. He was so natural, be it going left or right, hurling on his toes all the time. He had tremendous skill. It was always very, very hard to get past him.

★★★

RICHIE JNR

I WENT IN for senior panel trials in 2004 with Jamie; it was a Sunday morning after I'd played under-21 with Carrickshock the previous day, and I was playing corner-forward on Tommy Walsh. Jamie was playing wing-forward, facing Peter Barry.

Jamie is five years older than me, and he was a lot more seasoned than I was; I was very naive going into that trial, thinking that you would just go in and hurl like you hurl with your club. Tommy roasted me that morning.

I remember leaving James' Park and thinking, *Holy f**k, this is just a massive, massive step up.* There were high balls coming in and I was trying to sneak in behind Tommy to get the breaking ball… and no ball came. And there I was looking around… and Tommy was after grabbing it and was gone out the field.

This went on for the whole game.

It was just a disaster for me. But Jamie, on the other hand, played really well and was invited onto the panel, and that was fantastic. The whole experience gave me an insight into what it was going to take, if I really wanted to make it.

WE WERE AFTER winning the under-21 All-Ireland in 2004 in Nowlan Park, when we beat Tipperary quite comprehensively. And in December '04, both Jamie – who'd been on the senior panel that year – and myself both got phone calls. Jamie's call was to tell him that he was no longer part of the panel… and then I got a phone call inviting me onto it.

It's amazing, because the same thing happened with our clubmates John Tennyson (in) and Pat Tennyson (out) that same year. Two of us were in and the other two were told they were surplus to requirements. Talk about the highs and lows of sport.

A good crop of players from the 2004 under-21s were called into the senior panel in '05 – Cha Fitzpatrick, Tenno, myself and a few more – and I went straight into the starting team as corner-forward, which was fortunate for me. DJ Carey was full-forward and it all felt a bit surreal to me, because I grew up idolising DJ… and getting to hurl with him was beyond all my expectations.

The year started well for me and I felt I was holding my own. We got to the league final that year against Clare, though I was sick throughout the week leading up to it. I remember dad saying to me, 'Under no circumstances are you to play that game this weekend... because you won't be worth a shite'.

But that went in one ear... and out the other.

This was a league final, it was my first year on the senior panel and if I was picked, then of course I was going to play. I told Brian I was grand... then I went out, and I was shocking bad. I was marking Frank Lohan the same day and I was horrific. I ended up being taken off.

To this day, I still joke about it with dad, who was 100 percent right. I suppose being young and seeing it as your chance, you're kind of reluctant to give up the opportunity to start a final in your first year on the panel, to play and potentially win it... even if I'd been sick all week and drained of energy.

The moral of the story?

Listen to your body... and your father!

IT REALLY WAS a learning curve for me.

Come the championship, I started the Leinster semi-final, the Leinster final and the All-Ireland quarter-final against Limerick, but I was shocking poor that day and was dropped for the semi-final against Galway, which ended up being one of the crazier games of Brian's time in charge. We lost by 5-18 to 4-18.

I came on that day with a point to prove, thinking I shouldn't have been dropped and scored a couple of points. Again, dealing with not starting that match was another thing I had to digest. Most players come into the Kilkenny team having had an apprenticeship, having done their time as being a sub and being a bit-part player for big championship games. But that hadn't been my introduction and I've never lost sight of that.

Brian had obviously seen something in me that he felt I could bring to the team. But I had to take being dropped on the chin.

I know it's been said by others too, but I'd have viewed myself as being an unselfish player and there'd have been times when Brian would have told me that I was too unselfish. There were times when I should have possibly gone for my own score or been a little bit greedier and a little more direct – and dad would also have said that to me multiple times.

But I got as much satisfaction from setting up a goal or giving a pass for a point, than from scoring it myself. Hurling was never, ever an individual thing for me. It was never about me going out to see how much I could score, it was about going out and trying to help the team, and if I set up three or four points in a game and didn't score myself, then I was happy with that shift.

Not every player is like that, but that was always my approach.

That loss to Galway was a tough one to take, but it helped build the foundation for what was still ahead of Kilkenny under Brian. In fact, there's a good argument to be made that losing to Galway in '05 was the defining moment of Brian's term, and for us as a group of players. It made us young lads on the panel realise that we were going to get nothing without working as hard as we possibly could, both individually and collectively.

Going home on the bus after the Galway game, we'd stopped at an off-licence on the way and would have had a few drinks during the post-match meal. There were a few lads smoking down the back of the bus with the sunroof open, and that's where all the younger lads were… and I don't think that sat well with Brian all the way through to that December, when the preparations for 2006 began.

BUT BACK TO us down the back of the bus, and the setting of a different tone.

We were due to play Antrim in the under-21 All-Ireland semi-final the following weekend and we actually ended up going on the beer on the Monday, when we were supposed to be training that night.

I remember being called in to one-on-one meetings with Adrian Finan, the under-21 manager, on the Tuesday night… just to kind of air things out, and put it to bed. With that out of the way, we beat Antrim, so we were back into the final against Galway in Limerick, where we lost by a point (1-15 to 1-14).

In his *Kilkenny People* match report the following week, John Knox wrote… '*Galway went home celebrating wildly. Kilkenny went home full of repressed anguish'.* There was a picture of me accompanying John's report, on my haunches with my head in my hands. I'd had an absolute shocker. Two losses to Galway inside a few weeks wasn't what we'd hoped for, as the year ended on a disappointing note.

After the game, we went for a meal across the road and the next stop after that was the off-licence. We were all back onto the bus with boxes of beer, and I could sense that management weren't happy.

Now they didn't stop us from doing this, and they hadn't asked us not to either, but we drank the whole 67 miles home. When the drink starts to flow, the singing soon followed and there was a bit of craic on the bus… and plenty of laughing and joking. I don't think that sat well with the men at the top of the bus, and some feedback was probably relayed back to Brian and the senior selectors.

AT THE BEGINNING of 2006, my first All-Ireland senior winning year, the successful template for the decade that followed under Brian Cody was effectively laid out. We'd come in off the back of that semi-final defeat to Galway and they'd also beaten us in the under-21 All-Ireland… and our carry-on after both games didn't sit well with Brian. We met in the Hotel Kilkenny and everything was laid out for the year ahead, and what had gone on after we'd lost both the Galway games wasn't to be repeated.

The template for winning eight All-Irelands in 11 years was put in place at the start of that year. Cork were going for three in-a-row, which meant all the attention was on them, which was great for us. But every year, regardless of how we'd got on the previous year, the target was all about improving, how we could get to the top and what were we going to do to stay there. It was all about raising the bar that little bit higher every year, which we mostly did throughout that period. Regardless of whether it was one in-a-row, three in-a-row, or five in-a-row, the aim was to get back to Croke Park in September.

That was always the aim. To be there in the showpiece.

The question was put to us bluntly at that meeting… Were we, as players, hurting?

Were we upset?

I suppose our immediate reaction probably suggested that hadn't been the case. But having those questions put to us set the tone for 2006. It was incredibly business-like. The atmosphere changed. The mentality changed.

Everything was set out when it came to what was expected of us. That was the foundation that the four in-row was built on. And if you wanted to be in the senior team, there were standards that had to be met and maintained. Obviously, there was still some leeway to enjoy yourself outside of training and matches; we always met as a group on the Monday after a championship game and Brian never had any issue with that.

But once Monday had come and gone, it was back to basics and getting ready for a Leinster final or an All-Ireland semi-final and so on.

We had a mentality then that we were at the top of the pile, and we wanted to stay there. We never got sick of winning; the hunger never disappeared. In my mind, the way I always looked at it was… why would you go back and put yourself through December all the way to March with heavy training, unless you didn't want to be marching behind the Artane Band in Croke Park the following September.

The goal, always, was to be the All-Ireland champions and in my 11 years, that hunger never diminished. We knew if we had our house in order, it was going to take a seriously good team to knock us off our perch. I was lucky enough to enjoy so much success during my 11 years, but there were a few bumps along the road, more off the field than on in my case, of course.

There were times when I didn't really see eye-to-eye with Brian, and we would have clashed. And there were different times where a few of us would have stepped out of line off the field and we would have been pulled back in line. Then, obviously, taking my off the field stuff into account and, when you throw that into the mix as well, it makes it all the harder to perform at the highest level.

It's very difficult to get to that level when things aren't going well off the field; it makes it all the bigger of a challenge. But that's life.

It doesn't go in a smooth, straight line for too many of us all of the time.

I WAS IN St Pat's in Drumcondra the same time as Cha Fitzpatrick, and I'm not going to pretend that we didn't enjoy ourselves in Dublin. Take it from me, we did!

But Cha was able to do it and still train to a high standard. I wasn't. In 2005 or '06, Cha and myself were called into a meeting. This was after one week in particular when we went back to Dublin on a Sunday night, and Sunday to Thursday we spent every night that week in Coppers. We went home on the Friday and I think we were both pulled in for the meeting, and I was sat in front of Brian – he had obviously heard back about what was going on.

And I got asked about college, and was I enjoying it?

And sure, I said something along the lines of it going well, and having the odd night out here and there. He basically said that he knew myself and Cha were doing a good bit of drinking in Dublin, but then he mentioned how Cha could come back and train and be at the top of the running drills, and be standing out at training, while I was struggling.

So, I did admit to myself that something needed to change.

In the early days, when you're young, you think you can get away with it – that you can drink and train, and they're not going to know the difference. To a certain extent when you're young, you can get away with it, your body is able to take the night out and you're able to recover and go down and train… sweat it out, and be back to normal.

But I found it harder than Cha, because it was always a struggle for me to get to peak fitness.

There was never, ever a drinking ban in all the years I was involved. Brian never minded a lad going and having a few pints. There were times at home, if you went down to your local and had three or four pints, he didn't mind any of that.

He often said to us that at the end of the day, it's an amateur sport, number one. And the way he put it was family, work and hurling.

Family will always come first.

Your job is your job that you're going to have until you retire.

And then hurling is obviously a big part as well. So, it's all about balance. There was always times in college, if I ever felt under pressure with assignments or exams, you could always say it to Brian and you didn't have to come home on a Tuesday night for training.

Just as Kilkenny didn't do tactics, we didn't do drinking bans either.

Having the few drinks was a real bonding exercise in my eyes.

Throughout the league, there would have been very little drinking because you were still training hard and you were playing week in, week out. Now the odd time, when there was a two-week gap, the green light was there from Brian to go out on the Saturday or Sunday night and blow off a bit of steam… and then be back in on a Tuesday night and train hard. Lads used to be giddy about the prospect of going out.

And it was always the case then, after championship games, that we'd go for a few, regardless of winning or losing, on the Monday with the lads. It really was a case of… you win together, and you lose together. Those nights out were a reward, given the sacrifices you have to make when it comes to your social life and things you miss out on, like the 'afters' of weddings and so on. I mean, you could still go to them, but you knew you couldn't drink those nights.

Brian could see the reality of inter-county hurling as an amateur sport. It wasn't putting food on the table or anything of the sort. We had a management team that recognised that we were giving up a lot of our own time and making major sacrifices off the field – missing friends' weddings and so on – but you either wanted to make that sacrifice or you didn't. And that's the way we looked at it.

I was in a privileged position that with the group of Kilkenny players that I came through with and started my senior journey with in 2005. Even beforehand, with the minors and under-21s, we always knew – and again it wasn't a cockiness or an arrogance – but we knew that, if we could get our house in order, when we went back training in December or January, that we had a realistic chance of getting to an All-Ireland. And that was the pinnacle.

The weeks after the All-Irelands are the best memories that you can make, because you spend that whole week with the lads. But knowing when you went back to do the hard training in December or January, that you had a realistic chance of being there at the business end of the season, that's what kept you going.

★★★

RICHIE SNR

FOR A NUMBER of years, I would have felt that a lot of Kilkenny supporters might not have acknowledged the extent of Richie's contribution, because he mightn't come off the field with 1-3 or 1-4, or five or six points and a few frees on top of that. But his involvement in creating scores for others sometimes, I feel, went unnoticed.

He could have created four or five points for others, and someone might still have said after a match that Richie hadn't played all that well. But, sure, all he could do was shrug his shoulders when people said stuff like that.

He knew what he did, and he knew what he didn't do.

For me, having played senior, and having been there and done that, I could see what Richie had done on any given day. For me, it's extraordinary the amount of people that don't analyse the game the way I probably would in terms of passes and work rate.

It's an awful pity that the injury came when it did because I felt that Richie had three or four really, *really* good years left in him. He was getting over the hump in his life and I just felt that he was ready to explode for a couple of seasons. But then, along comes the injury which left him with no choice in the end; he had to call it a day.

Despite what was going on away from hurling for a period, he was still performing at a good level and then when he got a handle on things by 2014, we saw what Richie was capable of producing. If you weren't *producing* within that squad, he could have been sitting on the bench with the number 19 or 20 on his back.

The only All-Ireland final he didn't start when fully fit was in 2007 against Limerick. I remember coming in the back door at home the night the team had been named and Richie was sat in the kitchen, gutted.

I left him alone for an hour... he was in the sitting-room watching television, but I then came into him.

'Listen, turn off that telly now.

'I'm going to say one thing to you.

'You have two choices now... you can feel sorry for yourself and then go up to Croke Park next Sunday and, if you're called in, not perform.

'But what you've got to do now is get your head right... because you're going to play a part in this game at some stage.'

And in fairness to Richie – and I give him massive credit for it – he came in after 16 or 17 minutes into that final and he ended up having to take the frees because Henry Shefflin got injured.

I give him massive credit for that, because he was naturally disappointed at not starting. But when he came on, he took his opportunity well.

He must have said to himself beforehand that he was going to prove the selectors wrong if he got the chance.

And he did brilliantly that day.

★★★

RICHIE JNR

IN MY OFF-SEASON, I opted for complete downtime.

There wasn't a hurl picked up, there wasn't a gym visited or anything, or a field for a run or anything like that. I never did any fitness work on the team holiday or the All Star trips.

I remember seeing Seán Óg Ó hAilpín and a few more lads heading off for an early morning run, and I thought to myself... *Jesus Christ, what's he at?*

Now it didn't bother me in the slightest at the time, but it indicated where things were going at inter-county level and it truly set those lads apart at the time. And now it's become the norm. In the early part of my career, a few people would have said that I was a little bit lazy, but I feel I grew out of that as the years went by.

And I was a bit lazy when it came to hard training alright.

I really struggled with the hard slog, big-time. I don't think anyone genuinely enjoys pre-season. There's a time where you get to a level of fitness, where you don't find it as hard as it should be, as I felt it, but every year it was the same with me up until, ironically... when I was dropped at the end of 2013 and started training with Mickey Comerford. I got myself a base in that pre-season that I felt stood to me then over the next 18 months.

I'd sprint all day, I'd never had any issues with that, it was just the long-distance stuff that I hated. It's funny, I know a few players would have given interviews where they'd have been answering questionnaires about who would have been the worst trainer... and I would have been the answer to a lot of them plumped for.

And when it came to who was the 'moaniest' or something like that, JJ Delaney and Jackie Tyrrell would have mentioned me, so my name would have been around in public a bit when it came to 'me and training'. But to be fair, when the lads used to be asked who was the most skilful, my name was always in consideration when that question was put to them too.

I absolutely loved hurling.

But the training side of things was something I was never a big fan of. The 'application' that Eoin Larkin wrote about Henry Shefflin having, well that wasn't something I had in my armoury. I never cried off from pre-season training. It might have been a hell of a struggle to do it, but I always got through it.

We used to train hard on a Tuesday night in Kieran's and it was an absolute killer of a session each and every time. I remember coming in after one of the Tuesday night runs and, literally, just barely able to speak.

I'd worked out how many hours there was between then and the next Tuesday night run. We were sat in the dressing-room and we were all talking, when I said, 'Jesus, lads, it's only 166 and a bit hours… until we're back here for this again'.

The whole place erupted!

I suffered on those runs, but I liked to plonk myself in the corner, struggle to get into the shower – I'm not joking – and then try and bring a bit of craic into the dressing-room, because it was needed right after having the shit flogged out of us that evening.

You had to make a joke of it, to keep pushing yourself to come back to it the following week.

I look back on it now and realise, *Yeah, it was bloody hard.*

But was it all worth it in the end?

Absolutely. It got us to where we wanted to be eight times in 11 years. Mick Dempsey timed our training brilliantly, building our fitness and mood the whole way through the season. He was meticulous.

Mick's transition into the management team, having also been involved with Martin Fogarty with our under-21 team, was about as seamless as it could get. So having both of them come in with Brian, on the back of their familiarity with the players also making the step up, was huge. A lot of the players that came with them were among Kilkenny's stand-out performers for the following 10 to 15 years.

We knew them, they knew us… and it all worked so, so well. Those appointments really worked in our favour, and it was a huge help for me.

MYSELF, JOHN TENNYSON and Cha, as I've intimated, used to socialise a lot. We came up through minor and under-21, and we just clicked. About two or three weeks before the 2008 All-Ireland semi-final against Cork, when Cha was captain and we were going for three in-a-row, we ended up in Cha's homeplace in Knockmoylan and we decided to go down for a pint.

Anyone who knows the area will know how quiet it is.

We had two pints, and that was grand. Then we made the decision to go into the casino in Waterford, and pass a couple of hours in there. We had a few more bottles in the casino, spent a good bit of the night in Waterford and, then, we ended up at a house party in Kilmacow – and it went on all night, it was a 5 or 6am job by the time it finished up.

We got home eventually and, after a bit of sleep, I got myself ready to head back up to Dublin where I was working at the time.

I was coming down from Lucan (where I was living at the time) the following Tuesday for training, when Cha rang me.

'We were caught!' he says.

'What?' I said back.

'We were caught out on Saturday night!'

Cha had spent the whole day on Sunday on the beer, while Tennyson and myself had gone home. The whole way down to training, all I could think about was what was going to be said to us. *He's going to take the three of us to one side and give us a talking to.*

Cha and John were injured at the time, so I was the only one of the three of us that trained that night… and off I went.

The b*****ks was run out of us that night at training.

I remember running in off the field and thinking to myself, that if I run in and get changed… out the door and into the car… maybe there'll be nothing said.

I was showered, dried and nearly dressed, before any of the rest of the lads had even got into the shower… and I was heading for the door, and Brian was sat in his usual spot.

Just inside the back of the door.

'Richie!' he said.

'You might hold back there.'

'I want to see you.'

I'd a good idea what was coming – and the two boys had already been told. The dressing-room started to empty out, but the three of us were still there, with Brian and the selectors.

Brian said he'd heard what had gone on.

He wasn't roaring or anything like that.

He was talking away… and he started with Cha. He asked him what he was thinking, pointing out that he'd an opportunity to captain the county to three in-a-row, and so on.

He eventually moved on to 'Tenno' and myself, and pretty much said most of what he'd said to Cha back to us. I don't know if he was trying to make a joke of it, but Cha said to Brian, 'Jesus, Brian, if I wasn't a hurler or if I wasn't hurling, I'd be an alcoholic!'

The two of us started laughing… we really weren't expecting it.

Brian said to Cha that if he (Cha) wanted to drink rather than hurl, then he could always just concentrate on that.

Well, the mood quickly changed and it was left at that.

I firmly believe this and I've no problem saying it, and I said as much to Tenno… only for Cha was with us, I don't think either of us would have worn a Kilkenny jersey again under Brian Cody.

Brian was ruthless, and he was already after making some big decisions in the years before we came into the panel. Needless to say, the three of us kept our heads down for the following few weeks ahead of the Cork match, but to make matters even worse for myself, I was brutal in the semi-final and I was taken off about 10 minutes into the second-half, which didn't help the situation.

There was no big chat at home about any of this.

I was 23, and mam and dad's mentality was very much along the lines of me being big and old enough to make my own decisions. And if I'd made a decision that got me into trouble with the other lads, well then, I just had to own it and then get on with things.

I suppose that was, as a trio, the one and only time that we would have stepped outside the lines.

★★★

RICHIE SNR

THE KILKENNY TEAM Richie was a part of, all the way up to 2015… they just had a phenomenal group of players – they didn't really hurl to a game plan, at least not the way teams are doing now.

The same went for the Tipperary team of that era and just look at the quality of matches they served up in both the league and championship. Just incredible games, with only a puck of a ball between them in most big matches.

The 2013 qualifier at Nowlan Park, which we won by 0-20 to 1-14 will go down as the best atmosphere that was ever in the ground. It was a phenomenal occasion, and only for Lar Corbett getting injured that night, it would have gone right down to the wire.

There was so little to choose between those two teams during that era and they both brought out the best in each other. That was a massive Kilkenny team, and it'll tell you how good Tipperary were to come back year after year and bring them right to the wire.

It was a great time for both counties, and for hurling in general.

★★★

RICHIE JNR

BRIAN CODY'S LONGEVITY and success was incredible.

Year-in, year-out, he came back probably hungrier than the players. We knew we had a really good group of players. Brian did too and he got the best out of us. He stayed hungry and so did we.

It was a great combination.

You could essentially boil Brian's message down to this… effort, spirit and aggression… and then obviously you let the hurling take over.

If you brought those three qualities to every match, given the skill levels and stick work that was there too – and he knew we had that – you were always going to be hard to beat. The entire team had to work hard… your full-forward line was effectively your first line of defence.

That's what it took to succeed the way we did.

When Brian took over in 1999, his plan was to build a spirit within the Kilkenny dressing-room that couldn't be broken. His big thing was that there were 'players before ye' and there's going to be 'players there after ye'… so make sure ye leave the jersey in a better position than where it was when ye came into it.

And he firmly achieved that.

I can honestly say that throughout my 11 years with regards to however many players came through the set-up, we had a spirit that was unbreakable. We were willing to die for each other and that's a testament to Brian.

Did I leave the jersey in a better place?

Well, that's not for me to say.

But I hope I did.

WHEN I WAS driving down from Belfast and I knew my time was up because of the knee, I was on the phone to Brian and told him the diagnosis. He said to me that the reason he'd been hard on me at times – when I felt he was being too hard on me – was because he knew that the ability was there. He knew what I could do.

At the time, I kind of felt that he was being too hard on me and wished he'd go a bit easier. But having had that conversation with him at the end, it all made sense. Brian could see the potential that was there and he just needed to keep his foot on the pedal so that I could fulfil my potential. There were times where I took my foot off the pedal, and my standards dropped.

The level of performance always had to be high.

That's what Brian demanded, and what we as a group of players demanded. The training sessions at Nowlan Park underlined that. It was 'dog eat dog' stuff, lads laying into each other during the training matches and tackling drills. It was so raw.

It was as pure as hurling could get.

There'd be people watching on in the stands blown away by what we were doing. The physicality, the skill levels, the aggression... the pure fight.

While the injuries throughout my career have been well documented, I felt that any time I was fit, any time that I was ready to go, that I was part of Brian's plans. Whether that was because he saw something in me, or a trust or whatever, I don't really know, but I knew myself that if I was fit, I was I was ready.

If I was fit, I was going to play some part, I was going to be involved in some way or another, and that's how it materialised over the for the 11 years that I was there. That's not to say I wasn't dropped for big games.

I was dropped for the All-Ireland semi-final in 2005, I was dropped for the

All-Ireland final in 2007, and then I was dropped off the panel altogether for that spell in 2013.

I never took my place for granted or anything like that. I don't think anyone I played with ever did either.

★★★

RICHIE SNR

THE 2008 FINAL was, without doubt, Kilkenny operating at the peak of their powers under Brian Cody. But what Waterford did that day, before the game had even started, trying to rough up Kilkenny off the ball, was ridiculous. No one was going to beat that Kilkenny team by mixing with them like that.

It was a mind-boggling kind of day, with Waterford players doing stuff that they'd never done before in that arena and Kilkenny playing as well as any Kilkenny team ever had. Limerick's second-half in the 2023 All-Ireland is probably the only time anyone has operated at the same level in a final as Kilkenny did in '08.

Our bench that day was unbelievable: Richie Hogan, Michael Fennelly, John Tennyson, Michael Rice, James Ryall… and on and on. There were nine Kilkenny subs that day that would have been on any other team in Ireland that year. It was so one-sided there was no enjoyment in it.

If it had been tight for 40 or 50 minutes, and I'd say this of any game, at least that'd hold your attention… and well and good after that… whatever way the game would go.

I said that at half-time and a Kilkenny man near me looked at me in disbelief. 'What do you mean?' he said.

'Sure, where is the enjoyment in this? The game is over already,' I told him. 'Waterford haven't won an All-Ireland since '59 and look at the way the day has turned out for them.'

I was naturally delighted that we'd won another All-Ireland but that didn't stop me feeling sorry for Waterford either. If they'd got past Limerick in the semi-final the previous year, I think we'd have had one of the great finals, because that year was the best Waterford had been under Justin McCarthy. That team, with Ken McGrath, Dan Shanahan and John Mullane, sure it would have been brilliant to see them get over the line. It would have been huge for hurling. They were certainly good enough to win one, a bit like my own club in the 2013 senior championship, but to get over that line is so, so difficult.

The quality of the Kilkenny panel from 2007 through to 2012 was scary and I doubt if I'll ever see the likes of that again. And even Richie's young lad, who is in his early teens, I reckon he'll never see it again either. The lads from the under-21 teams I managed, who stepped into the senior panel, the standard they operated at so consistently for so long was just incredible... Noel Hickey, Michael Kavanagh, JJ Delaney, Tommy Walsh, Brian Hogan, Derek Lyng, Eddie Brennan and Henry Shefflin... it was phenomenal.

Limerick probably have a similar depth now, when you consider the way several players operated out of position in 2023 and it didn't diminish their quality at all. Similar to Kilkenny, about five to six years from now, this Limerick team will not be as dominant and the county may never have such a brilliant squad of players again for quite some time.

And when I think of my own lad, being part of that Kilkenny effort, to have started nearly every game in that period... giving 11 years and winning eight All-Ireland titles, it's a massive achievement.

★★★

RICHIE JNR

2008 STANDS OUT for a few different reasons.

We always felt that we were building towards a performance. Does a team or its manager ever feel that you'll deliver a complete performance?

I don't think so. As a manager, no matter how well your team has played, you always have to find faults to try and improve for the next day.

Don't get me wrong... the 2008 final was a performance to behold and something we're all very proud of, but we knew we had to improve for 2009. Otherwise, we wouldn't have gone and won the four in-a-row and stayed at the top of the table.

When Waterford beat Tipp in the semi-final, Davy Fitzgerald was carried out of the train in Waterford shoulder high and we were hearing a good few stories about the whole county going mad; sure they hadn't been in an All-Ireland final since 1963, so it was somewhat understandable.

What initially stood out on final day was taking to the pitch and every hair on the back of my neck standing up when Waterford came out onto the field. It's something I'll always remember. It felt like there were a million Waterford supporters in Croke Park that day given the phenomenal noise they made.

The way Waterford were set up became evident very quickly.

I remember myself, Taggy Fogarty and Eddie Brennan went into the full-forward line and the first thing the three lads in Waterford's full-back line did was dig us and dog us, and try to get us into a scuffle. It all felt a bit strange.

At the time you try and prepare for everything or anything, but you don't really anticipate that happening at the start of an All-Ireland final. You don't mind the lad marking you playing it tough or giving you the odd dig. But the Waterford lads were clearly looking for a full-blown… whatever!

And then we heard afterwards about the whole plan to cause a big scuffle all over the field – and apparently, at the other end, one of their forwards known for playing the ball was supposed to level Tommy Walsh and take him out of the game. I think everyone inside Croke Park was wondering what the hell was going on?

It was totally out of character for Waterford to take this kind of approach.

A few years later, on one of the trips, I remember speaking to one of the Waterford players about what went on at the start of the match and he said it was madness what the management had planned in the build-up to the match. And then it completely backfired.

Was that the reason we put the perfect performance together? Definitely not. We were building the whole time that year, we had improved through every game and everything just fell right, but Waterford's heads were gone after that scuffle. I firmly believe that their heads were gone after the first five minutes of that game. And then the game was over as a contest after 10 minutes and we ran out winners by 3-30 to 1-13.

I think Waterford were emotionally drained from the night before, from the whole build up to it, whereas we were preparing for our third final in-a-row, all doing what we regularly did – doing what we'd normally do on any Saturday.

Noel Hickey spent the Saturday night given an uncle of his down in Fiddown a hand on the farm. I was at home that night, slept in my own bed, got up the next morning and had breakfast with the family before meeting the rest of the panel and management and heading off to Croke Park.

The final came a year too late for that Waterford team. Had they beaten Limerick in the previous year's semi-final, I think we'd have had an epic final against them.

But that was our time.

★★★

ENDA McEVOY

FOR ME, RICHIE Jnr was, without doubt, the single most talented player during Brian Cody's era. TJ Reid came after him and has obviously been outstanding, but Richie was a fabulous hurler and had everything you could ever wish for, apart from one thing… a work ethic.

Richie was a big lad in his teens; he already had the frame of a player in his twenties and the word, going way back, was that this guy was a real chip off the block except more naturally talented than his father, and that he possessed nearly everything required to go right to the top very quickly.

And, had Richie possessed his father's work ethic, you'd be talking about one of the ultimate hurlers of any era.

Make no mistake, and I wouldn't want anyone suggesting otherwise, Richie Jnr was an outstanding hurler and a player of rare gifts. He was a senior inter-county before his 20th birthday.

Richie came on as a sub in the 2005 All-Ireland semi-final defeat to Galway (5-18 to 4-18) and in hindsight, Kilkenny were as well off losing to Galway because, had they got through, I suspect Cork would have beaten them in a second successive final.

And that could have meant the end of Brian Cody's time as manager… there would have been severe pressure had things gone that way, so they dodged a bullet by losing that day because lessons were learned after that Galway defeat.

Mick Dempsey and Martin Fogarty had just finished their first year alongside Cody. In '06, Kilkenny blooded a lot of young players, Jackie Tyrrell et al, with Richie starting and Cha in midfield, and everything changed for the better.

Richie Jnr's quality and the extent of his contribution to Kilkenny's success is undoubtedly underestimated. You have to remember, he played in a forward line where Henry Shefflin was the main man, Richie Hogan was there from '09, Eoin Larkin was always doing his stuff quietly, averaging two points a game, Martin Comerford was another highly effective and consistent performer, and then you had Eddie Brennan, who so regularly caught the eye – and then TJ Reid arrived onto the scene.

Initially, Richie didn't score the goals at the rate he did in the latter stages of his career and of course he came up with key goals in both the 2012 and 2014 All-Ireland finals against Galway and Tipperary. I do feel there's a constituency of people within Kilkenny who don't fully appreciate what a player we had in Richie either.

★★★

NICKY BRENNAN

WHILE RICHIE SNR NEVER had any real serious injuries, he was travelling all day as a rep, and then travelling again to get back for training. There was a fair old sacrifice attached to that. There were those couple of years that Richie and Ann were living in Cork, and they could well have stayed there and things, from a hurling perspective, would have been a great deal different for Richie and the youngsters that followed.

Given the job he had, the success he had in sales and the esteem he was held in by his colleagues, there was a distinct possibility that he could have stayed in Cork and young Richie could have been wearing a Cork jersey.

I'd say the thing that drew him back was his fierce allegiance to Carrickshock, and he's as devoted to the club now in many ways as he was while he was playing, through his work with the underage panels and in terms of club development. Because clubs just dream of having somebody like that, somebody who is a highly respected person in their locality, somebody who has achieved an awful lot.

He's not asking anyone to do anything that he hasn't done himself. He won his second All Star in '86 while he was chairing the club, which is an extraordinary achievement. But that's the mark of the man.

He just has huge passion for his own club… a passion for his own place and his county. I often wonder, going forward, will we get the same dedication from players once they're retired from playing?

RICHIE JNR

FROM THE OUTSIDE looking in, people would be thinking, *Jesus, he's after having some career.* And of course, they'd have a point.

I'd 11 years with Kilkenny, I played in nine All-Ireland finals – 11 in total including two replays – winning eight and losing only one.

But when I think about what I was dealing with off the field, from a personal point of view it could have been so much better – and I don't mean more All Stars or anything like that. Personal awards never bothered me. For me it was all about the team and it was what I could do to help the team, that's what I prided myself on.

Granted, from a team perspective, it'd be hard to imagine we could have been more successful than we were during that period.

VI

The
Management
Game

★★★

★★★

ENDA McEVOY

THE UNDER-21 ALL-IRELAND win in 1999 was very important for Kilkenny hurling, for two reasons. One, the seniors had lost to Cork in the Croke Park rain the previous Sunday, having also lost to Offaly in the previous year's All-Ireland final. It was also the day after PJ Delaney had been left fighting for his life in a hospital bed in Cork after he'd been attacked on a night out in Thurles. So, winning that under-21 title was huge, with Eddie Brennan, Henry Shefflin, Michael Kavanagh and Noel Hickey all featuring prominently, not knowing then what greatness lay ahead of them. In the build-up to the final, Richie Snr brought in Brendan Hackett, a sports psychologist, to talk to the players. It was a pioneering move for Kilkenny hurling.

★★★

RICHIE SNR

THE POWERS AND the Raggetts are two Carrickshock families that go back years and we've always had a great relationship; the brothers and myself hurled together with Brendan and Martin Raggett, and the whole lot of us are lifelong friends.

Brendan made his home in Carrickbeg, on the Waterford side of the boundary in Carrick-on-Suir, and that connection explains how I ended up managing the St Molleran's intermediate team in 1995, when the club won the county championship for only the second time in its history. Brendan, along with Tony Reade and Michael O'Shea, made up my management team and it was a very enjoyable two years down there.

'The Mollerans', as they're known all over Waterford, defeated Cappoquin 1-14 to 2-9 in the final at Walsh Park, the same opponents they'd got the better of 25 years previously when winning their first title.

Prior to that, I'd won a Kilkenny junior championship with Tullogher as well, so I'd gained a bit of managerial experience outside of my own club by then.

CARRICK IS ONE of the more interesting towns from a GAA perspective.

To have three clubs, two playing in Tipp, and one in Waterford, from a population of about 6,000 people – cross either of the bridges in Carrick and you're playing in a different county championship. It's extraordinary.

When you look at Kilkenny city, with 22,000-plus people and it has the same number of clubs as Carrick – James Stephens, O'Loughlin Gaels and Dicksboro – that's some statistic. And that's going to present a problem down the road for the GAA when it comes to Kilkenny city; there are houses being built on the Dicksboro side of Kilkenny at the moment and that's a club which is hardly able to cater for the young lads they have at present. It just makes you wonder where things are going to be in another 10 to 15 years' time.

Is the solution going to mean the foundation of a fourth city club and all the costs that'll arise from that? I'd suspect that's unlikely, in all honesty. The parish rule applies in Kilkenny, and again, I don't expect that to change either, but it's going to have to be looked at.

I've long been of the view that if we have people that were born and raised in their own parish and are living inside the city, and their young lads are not getting games, then why shouldn't they hurl with ourselves, or Clara and so on. There are good young players being overlooked by the city clubs on account of their numbers, so I think those players should be allowed to come back and play for their mother or father's home parish.

I think that's a practical solution. Having lads playing sport, whatever the code, is a brilliant activity to keep them engaged in something outside of school, especially if you're not too hot on the books and the study.

Very seldom you see guys that are playing football or playing hurling stepping too much out of line – and those that do, get brought back into line largely by the lads they're playing with. Being involved in sport is a second type of education, in its own way. I think it's hugely important to have kids involved.

And then, at the other end of the scale are people who just step away from the game completely, which still surprises me a bit. Their playing career might be over at the end of this year and then they mightn't be seen inside the gate of the field again for four or five years. But, thankfully a good few of them do come back in after they've been married, had a family… and a young player or two to bring in with them.

But I'd have found it hard to have had any sort of a break with the club. I guess I'm just not wired that way. I'd find it woefully hard, even when I'm just driving down through the street in Hugginstown and I'd just drive into the field for a look around… I mightn't even get out of the car. I just don't know how some people can switch off completely, but at the same time, everyone is different.

And I suppose for many people who are after giving so much of their lives to it, maybe there's just something else they've got more enthusiasm for and there's nothing at all wrong with that either.

I might have been, for a while, a bit too excitable on the line at underage with the lads maybe. And I'd say, if I were back now, I'd be way different. But I could go to a game now and sit there in the stand and take everything in.

That's what I love to do.

I love going off on my own to a game, and sitting on my own. I don't shout and roar at a game, I just sit there and take it all in. Obviously, there'd be days when you wouldn't be at a good game but that's part and parcel of it.

WHEN NICKY BRENNAN asked me to be one of his selectors with the Kilkenny seniors in 1996, I'd no hesitation in accepting the role. A county board official pulled me aside at the time and said to me, 'Will you not wait? Your own time will come!'

But the two years that I gave as a senior selector was an interesting experience. Now, 1997 was a very difficult year. I felt that some supporters within the county were critical of Nicky, given the fact that his brother, Canice was involved in the panel. I remember the All-Ireland quarter-final in '97 against Galway in Thurles – when we were nine points down at half-time – Pat Aylward and myself were abused from an individual in the stand that day.

And that was hard to take.

We'd brought on John Power at the break and we turned around and here was this fella, against the railing, roaring abuse at us. Nicky was down the sideline and I was hoping he wouldn't come back up towards us while that stuff was being said to us, as it would have been directed at him as well.

There's no place in the game for that. We were there doing our best for Kilkenny. Now we turned it around in the second-half, winning by 4-16 to 3-17 after one of DJ Carey's greatest ever performances, when he scored 2-8.

Come the full-time whistle, we heard nothing from the man who had been abusing us earlier but there was no great surprise in that. I knew who it was, he was a fella from South Kilkenny... and I met him about 18 months later and I was glad to be able to look him straight in the eye.

I don't think he was as happy to see me, as I was to see him!

★★★

NICKY BRENNAN

MY FIRST ENCOUNTER with Richie would have been beyond 1979, when I was back on the Kilkenny panel and we won the All-Ireland... and Richie, who'd be a few years younger than me, joined the panel in the early 80s and made such a big contribution to the 'double-double' win in 1982 and '83.

Ever since then, we've always been close and when I was asked to take on the Kilkenny senior manager's job in the mid-90s, Richie came on board with me. We'd been pally ever since we got to know each other through the Kilkenny set-up and regularly met up to talk about hurling. I'm close to a lot of the lads I'd have soldiered with, and myself and Richie often marked each other in training and we got to know each other fairly well that way.

Richie is incredibly well liked. Well, it's very easy to like him because he's not a messer, he's not a bullshitter.

The 1996 championship was the last year of straight knockout hurling. And obviously if you got beaten in that once, you were gone. We went into that '96 Leinster Championship meeting with Wexford down a few players and DJ Carey, who was taken off that day, had a leg injury which clearly impacted his performance.

We lost by 1-14 to 0-14 against the side which would go on to win the MacCarthy Cup so memorably against Limerick (1-13 to 0-14). We probably didn't play great that day but we were definitely hampered by injuries. A year later, we lost again to Wexford... and again we were missing players, but the back door had arrived and we played Galway in a famous quarter-final. We were down heavily at half-time and we were eaten out of it by a lot of Kilkenny supporters; there were fellas standing over either side of the tunnel, giving it to us big time.

We brought John Power on at half-time and we turned the game around... DJ Carey, who hadn't had a great day against Wexford, put on an exhibition in what was a fantastic match. We knew we were up against it in the semi-final against Clare... we'd lost Liam Simpson and Michael 'Titch' Phelan – a full-back and a full-forward – from the Galway game.

Clare were four points up after four minutes and we ultimately lost by four points, and that was naturally a huge disappointment.

We still had league matches to play and we ended up playing Limerick in a league semi-final in Nowlan Park... and the shit hit the fan that night.

The whole thing went pear shaped.

We lost by 1-17 to 0-10 and that was the end of myself, Richie and Pat Aylward as the management team... but I'd great trust in both of them. I was delighted with how we worked as a group, but it didn't work out for us.

That's how it goes, sometimes.

After that, I went down the administrative route and Richie kept coaching, and things didn't work out too badly for either of us.

Our period of involvement as Kilkenny's management was a completely different world now relative to the preparation around strength and conditioning, around nutrition, around the whole sports science end of things. I mean, things were still relatively archaic in the mid-90s. It probably started to come in the early part of the 2000s.

We played in an era, Richie and I, where your training was done in Nowlan Park and whatever you did on your own, you did it on your own. You didn't have anything like the back-up services that are now attached to every team. So maybe in some respects, you depended on individuals at that stage to manage the whole process, whereas now you have armies of background people who advise senior managers about various aspects of player preparation, which is a completely different scene from where it was when we were both playing and involved in team management.

Going into the Kilkenny job, I felt it was going to be a period where we were probably going to introduce several players, but ultimately hand them on to someone else. But I felt we just didn't get the rub of the green at all in either year. Injuries really hampered us and in both those years we lost to the eventual All-Ireland winners in their respective golden eras.

Looking back on it now, it obviously wasn't a great period for Kilkenny, but in the context of hurling, it probably wasn't bad for the game. And while Kevin Fennelly didn't last too long after our time, players like Andy Comerford and Peter Barry and Philly Larkin made a big impression in the early years of Brian Cody's reign and brought home a first All-Ireland in seven years in 2000... and, of course, an incredible era followed.

★★★

RICHIE SNR

BY THE TIME I got the Kilkenny under-21 manager's position, the fact I'd won that county final with St Molleran's in '95 meant my name was out there and I was delighted to get the Kilkenny job. That meant a lot to me.

In the autumn of 1998, I put my name forward for the Kilkenny senior manager's job, the year that Brian Cody was ultimately appointed, but I've got to be honest... I don't think I would have been good enough to do that job. I just don't think I'd have been cool enough.

Now maybe I might have adapted to what it demanded, but would you get the time to learn in a job like that, in a county like Kilkenny? I really enjoyed my three years with the Kilkenny under-21s, and the fact that Jamie was involved when we won the All-Ireland in '99 made it extra special.

I think the Kilkenny job demands a certain type of an individual to take it on and handle everything that goes with it. Now, Richie could be that, looking down the line. There could be abuse thrown at Richie and I don't think it would get to him… it'd be like water running off the duck's back with him.

Whereas with me, I'd have been different.

If things weren't going well, I think it'd get in on me. You have to be so strong in that job, when it comes to all the slings and arrows of inter-county management. And I'd definitely say that managing the Kilkenny senior team is one of the more pressurised jobs at inter-county level given the level of expectation there is most years.

Some people can thrive on that. Pat Henderson and Ollie Walsh did in my time and, of course, Brian Cody obviously and most spectacularly did too.

Of course, there's always a bit of 'What if' at play… if the board had gone for me instead of Brian? But on the whole, I think it was a blessing in disguise that I didn't get the job. I'd have been so engrossed by the job that, if it hadn't worked out for me, I don't think I'd have been able to put it out of my thoughts away from training and matches.

If you have a bad day, you've got to look forward to the next day as soon as you can after the full-time whistle, to try and get things right. Don't get me wrong… it was an honour to be asked to put my name forward, but I think history has shown that the county board made the right appointment in November 1998.

WHEN BRIAN GOT the job, he'd probably had 10-to-12 years of experience training James Stephens, without any great level of success, so you could say that the county board took something of a gamble too in appointing him. But the way it worked out was phenomenal – it will never be seen again in the county.

He came in after the low ebb of losing the '98 All-Ireland final to Offaly and while we lost the final again the following year in a downpour to Cork, things came good in 2000 when we hammered Offaly, and that set the ball rolling for an incredible run of success.

The night I got the phone call to tell me I hadn't been successful in applying for the senior job, John Healy, the county board chairman at the time, asked me would I put my name forward for the under-21s. So I did, and a week later I got the job and I really enjoyed the following three years. I had Murty Kennedy, John Marnell and Eamon Hennessy alongside me in management and we got on like a house on fire.

And things ended up working out very well for us.

Before the 1999 final against Galway, I made the decision to bring in a sports psychologist to the lads. I didn't realise at the time that this probably put me ahead of the curve, given the prominence of sports psychology throughout inter-county set-ups nowadays. But at the time, I felt another voice wouldn't do the lads any harm at all, so I asked Brendan Hackett, who had coached the successful Irish Compromise (International) Rules in Australia in 1990, to speak to the panel.

Brendan had been brought in to talk to the Rathnure hurlers in Wexford earlier that year – and they were being managed by my good friend, John Conran at the time – and the thought of asking Brendan in had been stuck in the back of my head for a while. I reckoned there was nothing to lose by bringing Brendan in before the final.

I ran it by the selectors and collectively we decided to bring him in. I had the Tuesday before the All-Ireland final in mind for it all, so I rang Brendan, explained how I got his name and he agreed to it. I was of the view that any bit of help we could get, to help get the lads over the line in the final, was worth going after.

I don't think the county board were overly happy with me, but I went to the Kilkenny Supporters Club and they sorted me out. What we did is now part and parcel of the modern game.

We went to Tullamore that Tuesday – where the final was going to be played. This was two days after the seniors had lost the All-Ireland final to Cork and we'd had two players on that panel, Henry Shefflin and Michael Kavanagh. We sat down with the two lads on Tuesday morning and told them we were heading to Tullamore that evening and while we didn't expect them to tog out, we wanted them to travel with us because we were going to have a meeting in the Tullamore Court Hotel after the run-out in the field. And they both travelled.

They both showed some serious leadership that particular week – and it wouldn't be the last time they did that. After training, as we were going into the meeting room, Eddie Brennan asked me, 'What's this all about?'

'Look, just head in, sit down and see what you think,' I replied. So, Brendan took the floor and we listened.

A new face, a new voice, coming at things from a slightly different angle.

In 1998, Brendan had written a piece in the Kilkenny GAA Yearbook, headlined 'Success from Within', which was the title of the book he'd published that same year. To me, Brendan spoke a great deal of sense, and it's a role he has maintained to this day, having enjoyed All-Ireland minor football success with Kildare, and he also led Ballymun Kickhams to the 2020 Dublin senior football title.

'Commitment tends to be stronger when it comes from within. Although in gaelic games there are still some powerful external motivations, such as the pride in club and county. With commitment, it is a case of actions speak louder than words. You often have to train when you would rather do something else. You may have to follow training programmes you don't like. You will need to stay positive when those around you are often negative. Above all, you've got to prepare thoroughly for those rare moments of success...

'The habits of training are carried onto the field of play. If you are negative, uncommitted, lazy, distracted and unfocused in your training, it will be very difficult to be in a mental state that is conducive to playing well on the day of a match. So the message is to be aware of your mind as you train and you should be conscious of developing your mental fitness as you prepare for your sport.'

Brendan's message went down well with the lads.

He stressed that it was only a game and it just had to be treated the same way as any other game. Brendan didn't want the lads to be fixated on the game... morning, noon and night for the week and he encouraged us to avoid talking about it at home, which was no mean feat in our house since Jamie, our eldest, was the Kilkenny goalkeeper that year!

But we stuck to that advice well; we weren't sat at the kitchen table every spare minute going through what we'd be doing the following Sunday.

'Whatever happens by the full-time whistle, make sure you walk off that field with no regrets,' Brendan said. 'And even if it goes against you in terms of the result, as long as you know you left everything out there, then you'll know you've stayed honest to yourself... and your teammates.'

I was delighted we'd done it.

I was always in favour of doing everything possible to put lads in the best frame of mind before a big match. And given that we'd just lost the senior final, the mood around the county was naturally low... so the chat put the whole group in a positive frame of mind. It was all about getting them all into a good mindset ahead of the final.

We knew we were going in as underdogs. But we saw it out that Sunday in Tullamore, beating Galway by 1-13 to 0-14 and it was a great one to win given the seniors' disappointment in Croke Park the previous weekend. And that same evening, Eddie Brennan came over to me and said: 'Well, I know what that talk the other night was all about now'.

Jamie said something similar to me. 'Well, it was definitely something different. It's not as if he had us sat there for two hours either.'

THE WAY THINGS turned out, it was fantastic having Jamie in goal, winning an All-Ireland. Initially, I wasn't beating a loud drum to bring him in as he'd just come off the '98 Kilkenny minor team. The fact that I was the manager was a position I didn't really want to be in, in terms of having my own lad involved in the panel. But about two-to-three months into the season, we felt were in trouble when it came to the goalkeeper, so one morning, the rest of the management team sat me down in Langton's before a challenge in Thurles against Tipperary, and they recommended we bring in Jamie, play him that morning and, if it didn't go well, we'd move on and wouldn't bring up his name again. I agreed, so we brought Jamie along, we played out a cracking game with Tipp and he had played very well. We left Semple that day confident that we had a squad that could win the All-Ireland title. Jamie had justified his call-up and he played his part in us getting over Galway. He was exceptional. And he wasn't the only one.

Noel Hickey was our captain at 19 years of age, and was already developing into a commanding full-back. And just look at what he went on to achieve as a senior hurler, becoming the outstanding player in his position for the decade that followed. Then you had Michael Kavanagh, Derek Lyng, Sean Dowling, Richie Mullally, Eddie Brennan and Henry Shefflin, of course. Great, genuine lads, who never shied away from hard work.

The following year, Brian Cody brought in six or seven lads from that under-21 group and what they went on to achieve was just incredible. We never saw anything like the team that swept all before them for most of the next 16 summers. And if we live to see such success again in Kilkenny, we'd be a very lucky generation of supporters.

My God, the satisfaction they gave us for so, so long. Just brilliant.

To have managed those lads, given how well so many of them did afterwards, was hugely satisfying for us as a management team. That's what a minor and under-20 manager dreams about... seeing lads you've trained along the way going on to be everything you'd hope they'd be.

Here's a good one about Eddie Brennan… I was walking up John Street one Monday evening, about three months into training and this man asked me how I was getting on with the under-21s. And sure, I told him we were going well and that we were getting fierce commitment from the lads.

'But if we could find another forward, that wouldn't do us any harm.'

'Wait 'til I tell you,' he replied. 'There's a lad playing junior with Graigue Ballycallan and, Richie, I'm telling you now… he'd be well worth going to have a look at. I can't understand how he's not on their senior team.'

The following Friday evening, Graigue were playing Dunamaggin in Callan and my God, Eddie was on fire that night. I came home that night, rang each of the management team and said we're going to have to look at this lad.

We did, and we brought him in.

Eddie scored 3-7 in our four matches, including our only goal in the final against Galway. He'd go on to score 26 senior championship goals, winning eight All-Ireland titles, 10 Leinster medals, four National Leagues and four All Stars. And he only ever lost one Leinster Championship match during his playing career… in 2004, against a Wexford team managed by my friend John Conran.

AROUND THE TURN of the century, I gave two years with Castletown, training them in the Laois Senior Championship. Luckily enough, we won the championship in both years (they've won eight in total) and I think, at the time, I held the record for the manager who lasted the longest in Castletown! The passion for hurling in the people I met in Laois runs as deep as anywhere in the country – and the Castletown lads I managed would go to the ends of the earth to win a match.

Pat Phelan, a man I used to meet while I was on the road for the job through that part of the country, came down to me one evening and told me they were looking for a manager.

'You won't have any trouble!' he promised.

'There's one or two lads that might need a bit of looking after, but the rest of them are brilliant.' He talked me into it and off I went, and we ended up in the 2002 county final in my first year and that set the ball rolling well for me.

I went up to Castletown on my own – I didn't go in with a management team with anyone I knew well from Kilkenny. If I was doing it now, I think I'd definitely have someone coming with me. You'd just have to be that bit more professional about it. In 2002, we were in a brilliant position to beat Birr in a Leinster semi-final but, just before half-time, we conceded four points and they just got out ahead of us in the end. The following year, having retained the senior championship, we came down to Nowlan Park to play Birr again, in the Leinster final this time, and going into it I thought we were really ready for it. But Birr, one of the great club sides of that era, beat us by 4-17 to 1-9.

They blew us out of the water. The following year, I had a feeling I'd got as much out of the lads as I was going to get. I tried to add in a couple of young lads early on in the year but I don't think that went down too well with some of the older players, which was disappointing. I got the sense that it was time to move on, after a few players came to me after a league match early on in the year in Rathdowney, after I'd played a couple of young lads and being told that these young lads weren't good enough. So, I made up my mind that when that year was over, I'd be done and dusted.

That was the only time players ever approached me like that. Whatever I asked the Mollerans lads to do, they did… and the same with Tullogher; I got a massive response out of them when I went down for the year in 1997.

I really enjoyed my time with Castletown. I remember us beating Ballinakill on a Saturday evening in Portlaoise to reach a county final. When the final whistle went, I called the three selectors and I said to them, 'Now lads, we're training tomorrow morning at seven o'clock. We wouldn't win a county final the way we hurled today'.

'Richie!' one of them replied quickly. 'There's no way you'll get these lads here at seven tomorrow morning'.

I went into the dressing-room and said we'd have a few words when they were showered and togged in. 'Right, lads,' I said, 'I want everyone in the field tomorrow morning at seven o'clock'. There was silence for a couple of seconds.

'This has to be done, lads.

'If we want to win this county final, then we have to be in the field tomorrow morning. We have to be willing to go do that.'

The following morning, it was All-Ireland final day, and I was gone three miles up the road when Suzanne told me she was after forgetting her shoes. So, I had to turn around, come back and grab the shoes… and when I ended up in the field at Castletown there was 27 lads there… at five past seven. The club chairman had organised breakfast for us in Mountrath after a really good training session.

We bonded well that morning and we ended up hurling really well in the county final. I'm sure the lads had something else in their minds after the final whistle on the Saturday night, but to see them all there, to a man, the following morning at that hour, was a great sign. It gave me the belief that these guys really wanted to go the extra mile.

I'd meet a good few of the lads still from time to time, and it's always nice to see them and hopefully the club can get back to where it was in the late 90s and early 2000s.

I'M VERY PROUD of the fact that I had success with all of the clubs I've been involved in. For me, it all boils down to being honest with players and trying to get the best out of them. The only regret I would have had about my own club – and I think I might have said this already – is after giving years with the under-13s, 14s, 16s and 18s, I decided to go with the under-21s and I know, looking back on it now, that it was a mistake.

Looking at it now, some years later, they needed a new face and a fresh voice which could have brought that group on another step. But to have only the one regret from a managerial perspective probably isn't too bad at this stage of my life.

I gave a couple of years training our own lads in the senior championship and I was happy enough with how that went, as we'd just come up out of intermediate, and in 2006, our second year up, we pushed the Shamrocks to a point in a quarter-final before they went on and won another county final along with Leinster and All-Ireland titles. But between my time hurling with the club, and my sons' time hurling with Carrickshock, we probably should have won more.

Why we've not had that level of success, I'm not sure.

Is it down to us being a little bit like a county that's not used to winning, that we've found it so difficult to get across the finish line?

Over my time and with the lads I hurled with, we had a great attitude in the club. We had great lads to train. There was no one acting the maggot and everyone was there to do their best. I know we had great times and you have to enjoy the wins when you get them.

Being a manager now requires a lot of demands and expectations that didn't apply when I began managing. If a club approached me in the morning and asked would I be interested in managing them, the first thing I'd say to that guy… or I'd say to myself, is this, and this goes for most clubs at this time.

I'd probably have eight or 10 players in college in Dublin, Cork, Limerick and so on, and they're seeing the way training is being done in colleges – though it might not be any better than what I'd come up with. But I'd probably be classed as old fashioned in the eyes of many younger players nowadays. And it's so important, as a manager, that you bring your players with you.

There's a lot of things going on in training grounds now and maybe there's no need for it – all the cones that are used pretty much everywhere now, for example. At the end of the day, it's about your first touch. Get yourself fit and get your first touch right, and if you have those right then I think you'll stand in with anyone.

But you will not maintain a standard or improve your level if you're not in the training ground, working on your touch. Tommy Walsh is hurling away in midfield for Tullaroan all the time and his first touch is still outstanding. And it's still that good because he's never stopped working on it.

As a manager, you have to keep things fresh, which is something Richie kept in mind going into his fourth year with the club as manager, when he brought in Niall Williams from Wexford to introduce a new face and a fresh voice. It's a fierce commitment.

When I was training Tullogher, the Mollerans or Castletown, there was no such thing of going into a group of players and telling them I wanted them off the drink for the next six weeks. You just went in and asked for a bit of cop on, two or three weeks out! Today, management teams are looking for players to stay off the drink for two to three months while the championship is on.

It's an amateur game. Managers also have to look out for players whose lives mightn't be as comfortable for them as other players – and every club has a couple of them – so you have to be able to work with them too and deal with that as well.

The job spec for inter-county players has changed a lot too.

There's not many full-time farmers involved in senior set-ups now because it's so difficult to try and balance work with family life and training. You could have a really good hurler who might be working at the home farm and he'll soon know what needs to be looked after… above everything else.

The commitment level required now at senior level is definitely ruling out lads due to the day job and, if you're on a farm, you're talking about a lot of unavoidably long days. Have things gone too far?

That's a question I've found myself asking more and more over the last few years.

LEAGUE MATCHES ARE now starting at the end of January or early February and, from there until All-Ireland final day, before they've even a ball pucked with their clubs, it's go, go… go… for the most competitive counties. It's some demand on the body. But it can't be forgotten that we're still talking about amateur players.

Every one of them is up on a Monday morning for work, be it on a building site, a farm or in an office to pay a mortgage. The round robin system appears to be bedding in well, but it is putting some demand on senior hurlers.

In my time, when we came out of a Leinster Championship match against Offaly or Wexford, the body was sore for two or three days afterwards. Now, they're in on a Tuesday after playing on a Saturday evening or Sunday afternoon to get ready for another championship match the following Saturday or Sunday. I think there should be two weeks between every championship match.

It's great to see so many games being played on drier pitches, but I feel it's too condensed; and the new championship structure has made a shambles of the league. I think we're very close to a stage where only the die-hard supporters will head out to watch a league match, particularly after the last two years.

It's just shadow-boxing and players, at least from what I can see, are not ready to perform when it comes to the league; all the early season focus is on physical training with the championship in mind. Maybe the league needs to be streamlined a bit so that the championship can start two or three weeks earlier than it currently is?

For players of my generation, the league was fierce important.

Every year we looked at the league and had only one thing in mind… to try and win it. I won five leagues and they were hard earned, and we loved to win it and to be competitive in it. It was a major competition at that time. It got going in October and November, and that was a great time for a player maybe that was coming onto the scene, to get a couple of matches. Because you still had your big-hitters in the club championship – the Shamrocks and James Stephens of this world – fighting it out in the championship before the Leinster club campaign and that tied up a few front-line players.

Once we went back in after Christmas, you'd still have three or four league matches left to play, and every one of them were big games. But the league's problem now is that it's too near the championship. It has no room to breathe in its own right as our second national hurling competition.

I think the league has lost its appeal. I don't think it means anything to counties like it did when I was hurling. The Walsh Cup and the Munster Senior League and these other pre-league matches… they should be scrapped now.

One suggestion put out by Michael Foley of *The Sunday Times* before the conclusion of the 2023 championships was to run the hurling and football championships separately, in separate halves of the year. Both All-Ireland finals are now in July and then we enter total shutdown in terms of inter-county action until the following January. TG4 has done a brilliant job covering club games and there's a lot of streaming packages after being developed, but maybe there is a case for dedicating the first half of the year to one code, and then the second half to the other. If you finished the hurling by mid-July, the football could be finished by the middle or the end of September, and then the biggest matches in either code aren't almost running into each other the way the senior hurling and football finals currently do.

It'd probably give the GAA a better chance of promoting the Joe McDonagh Cup and the other tiered hurling competitions, along with the Tailteann Cup. And if you did stagger things a bit like that, you'd be expanding media coverage as well and it might defuse a lot of the GAAGo controversy if we didn't have quite so many games scheduled pretty much on top of each other. Dual counties probably wouldn't be too hot on this suggestion and that ultimately might be the biggest stumbling block. I still think it'd be worth looking at.

THE RAILWAY CUP used to fill Croke Park, but the last final played in 2016 didn't break the 600 mark… and it's gone now. Time moves on.

The one regret I have in a hurling sense is that I never won a Railway Cup having played in a couple of finals. I was lucky and honoured to be picked a few times with Leinster and we really enjoyed it. I then gave four years as a selector with Brian Whelahan and John Conran, and we won it three times – in 2006, '08 and '09.

I thought it was great, because it gave you the chance to hurl with players you've been at war against for years in Leinster. And it's amazing the way you'd develop relationships with some of the lads.

John Conran and myself had heaps of battles when Kilkenny were playing Wexford in Croke Park, but we became great friends. I'd be good friends with Offaly's Pat Delaney, but that friendship developed on account of playing with Leinster. It was great to get to hurl with the likes of John Taylor and Niall Rigney from Laois and a few lads from Westmeath. The Railway Cup provided those counties with a chance to put forward some of their players to hurl in more competitive teams against the best players from the other provinces.

Where you'd fit the Railway Cup back in now would be the thing, of course. Maybe you pick provincial panels from counties out of the championship and have the final before the All-Ireland senior final and then you're giving some players a day out in Croke Park that realistically they'll never have otherwise at the senior grade.

FOR ALL THE physiotherapy and rehab that's available now, there are probably more players breaking down than there were 20 or 30 years ago. There are players in every county who are now missing most of the season. Is that down to all the hard training they're doing?

Is the body just not able for it?

Are all these soft tissue injuries the body's way of telling the player... you're flogging me to burn-out?

I knew one lad who was on the fringes of the Tipperary panel about five or six years ago and he was getting out of the bed at 5:15 in the morning to go to Dublin to work, then back to Thurles that evening... grab his gear, and get up to Semple Stadium for training. And he was left with a big decision to make.

He told me one evening that he just couldn't keep doing it. The body was breaking down and his job was suffering. 'Look, we all love the game,' I said to him. 'You can always go back and hurl with your club until well into your thirties, if you're lucky enough. But the job has to be number one.'

He made the decision, and withdrew from the 32-man panel.

Who knows, he may well have ended up in the first 26 or even the starting 15, but he just couldn't keep living the way he was.

There's just such a massive demand on players nowadays and it makes me wonder when someone is going to cry halt to this and say… enough is enough. It's such a huge element of your life. Don't get me wrong… I doubt that Richie, Jamie, John or myself would do things differently, if we had our time over again with hurling, but it's after going up a few notches again since Richie retired.

An amateur game played in a professional environment isn't a great fit.

I'd do very little with a team in the week leading up to a game because if you haven't the work done by then, you're in trouble. Of course, a lot of it is in between the ears, but if the body is right coming into a match, that's the ideal mindset to have before the ball is thrown in. And of course, rest is even more important when you're training minor and underage players.

I felt what I put in place worked for all the players I dealt with. I always did my best to act in their best interests. Decent rest ahead of a big match is so important for every player. A player will not play better if he's flogged in training in the build-up to a match.

★★★

RICHIE JNR

GETTING INVOLVED IN coaching was never about filling a gap once I'd stopped playing. I was always going to give something back to the club, whether it was at juvenile, minor or beyond that.

I always felt that I was going down that route.

Now, there'd be some people out there who might think that just because you hurled for your county and won All-Irelands, that that playing success will automatically make you a great coach. There have never been any guarantees on that front, and I for one never felt that way about it. I just wanted to give it a go. So, my first coaching role was with the Offaly camogie team and that was followed by a spell with the WIT Freshers' panel. I enjoyed my time with both and that's what put me into the starting blocks when it came to coaching.

Hurling was always going to be a huge part of my life, regardless of what I did or didn't take on once I'd stopped playing. And then, at the end of 2019, along came the Carrickshock job. Did I know it was coming? Absolutely not.

In October 2019, Gowran beat us in the first round of the intermediate championship by 19 points in Thomastown, and I remember walking out of the field that evening and it really felt like a low ebb for the club. By the following March, Covid-19 arrived and turned all of our lives upside down.

The manager had finished up by then and the club was looking for a successor, so the chairman approached me and asked me would I be interested in taking it on. It wasn't an automatic yes. I really thought long and hard about it… because I'd played with all these lads.

No different to dad and the rest of the family, I'm very, very passionate about Carrickshock and I owe an awful lot to the club. Everything, really. When you take on a job like that, you're not going into it to be liked; you're not going into it to try and make friends or anything like that.

You're going in to do the right job, and I had to make a decision about whether I was prepared to do that. I was going to be managing two of my brothers, cousins… young lads that I'd hurled with. And this was going to be a job where I knew I'd have to be ruthless – and I made that very clear from day one.

I also told them that at the end of the year, I hoped that I could sit down and have a pint with everyone and that we'd be able to look back on the year and have the laugh and the craic. However, my message was crystal clear…

'But at the end of the day, lads, I know that's not what I'm here for.

'That's not what I'm here to do.

'I'm here to do a job that's going to benefit Carrickshock.'

I won't make any bones about it. When I took on the job, we were in a fierce bad way. We were seriously looking at being relegated down to junior.

Some things in the club had turned a little bit toxic, and one or two things had happened in previous years, such as getting rid of a manager at a certain stage that I wasn't happy about. I had numerous conversations with dad about taking on the job. I really thought long and hard about it, and it wasn't a case of me jumping at the opportunity. I obviously looked at the result against Gowran, I looked at the players we had and what direction the club was going in.

I was home one evening with dad after having a few drinks, and we both agreed that my main ambition as manager was to keep Carrickshock in the intermediate championship. That was the big goal.

We knew we had underage players coming and it really was a case of keeping us at intermediate until this next wave broke through. My feeling was that if we maintained our status while integrating these players, that would put us at a level where we'd be a comfortable intermediate team.

Did I think we'd survive senior at that time? I didn't think we would. My goal for year one was to keep the club up; year two was all about building on the previous year – we got to a quarter-final and then year three had to demonstrate a further improvement – which we achieved by reaching the semi-final. Then, bigger ambitions for year four, although year four turned out to be more difficult than any of the preceding seasons. Initially, it wasn't an easy decision to make and I had plenty of other offers on the table from several teams that would have contacted me about coaching and managing or being involved at other levels.

WITH CARRICKSHOCK, I knew I was going in as manager and coach, which is an undertaking in itself – and you're doing all of that with the club you grew up in. I've always said… it's much harder to manage and coach your own club than another club. Just say I was involved with Ballygunner or Mount Sion in Waterford or Mount Leinster Rangers in Carlow, for example, and you'd go in on a Friday night and have a bad training session… you get in the car after it, and drive out the gate of their field.

Your own club gives you sleepless nights… wondering where we're going. What are we doing right? What might we be getting wrong? And I knew this was going to be the case when I took it on. Some people can compartmentalise things, whereas that wouldn't be me.

When it comes to Carrickshock, I'm all in.

Your own club is the be-all and end-all. And whatever role may lie ahead for me elsewhere in the future, that belief and devotion will never change.

To me, taking on the job when I did, felt like a massive task because not too many people walking out of the gate in Thomastown after we'd taking a pasting would have put their hand in the air. In December 2019, before Covid arrived and took hold, our under-21s went down to play a Roinn 'C' county final against Slieverue, and with about three minutes left on the clock, we were two points down. But the lads came back to win it by a point thanks to three scores from play.

And I said it to them afterwards, that that was the day I decided to take the job. Up until that performance, I was still undecided. But to be standing on the field, looking at the celebrations, looking at the lads accepting the cup, it really felt to me like there was *something* there. From there, it was all about assembling the management team and getting to work.

The first thing I felt I had to do was to bring a positive culture into the club and introducing young lads onto the panel. It's not that we were a particularly old team or anything like that, but I felt the group needed a fresh injection. Originally, I had a two-year plan in mind; to calm the ship and make sure that we were still an intermediate club in two years' time… and then benefit from the presence and pace of the younger players, and that they'd drive on things from there.

In year one, with the championship structure quite different due to Covid, we had an okay season. We won quite a few games but then we got caught in the first round of the championship which put us into a relegation semi-final. And whenever the word 'relegation' is mentioned in our club, it tends to lead to a sense of panic. But I didn't feel that way at all. I knew we were after hurling really well that year and we ended up winning that semi-final in Clara against St Patrick's by 0-17 to 0-13, when Michael Rice and Jamie came up trumps for us. But that was the end of that season for us.

The following year brought further improvement when we reached another quarter-final, which we mostly controlled against St Lachtain's at Nowlan Park; we were six points up at the second water break but between then and full-time we were outscored by 1-7 to 0-1. So that brought an end to my two-year term, though the team was in a better place, and I felt I'd done my bit. But then, having had a chat with the players, the captain approached me and said they wanted me and the rest of the management team back.

I went home to Maria, had a chat with her about it and decided I was going to give it one more year. There was definitely a feeling of unfinished business as far as I was concerned. We put a massive effort into year three, in 2022, and went one step further when reaching the county semi-final on a wet day against Thomastown, who would have been promotion favourites over the last number of years… and again, we came up that little bit short, losing by 1-14 to 1-10.

After the match, I gave a speech in the dressing-room in which, more or less, I said that I was stepping aside and I thanked everyone for their time and effort over the three years we'd had together. The months went on and I must have had anything between 20 and 30 phone calls, including a couple of inter-county set-ups, but I was still undecided about what I was going to do when it came to Carrickshock.

I had another conversation with Maria about it and I think she was a little surprised. After the semi-final against Thomastown, I felt we had left it behind us and then I went to the county final afterwards, which Danesfort won after extra-time (1-36 to 4-25) and I was fully convinced that if we'd got past Thomastown, that we'd have won the final. If we'd been beaten out the gate by Thomastown, I wouldn't have given another year a second thought.

One or two mistakes cost us massively that day and that was a game in which hardly anyone outside the parish gave us any sort of a chance. But we had Thomastown on the ropes.

The other thing that occurred to me a lot later was the circumstances which had led me to be appointed in the first place – losing to Young Irelands in 2019.

It wasn't a massive consideration but maybe something in my subconscious told me that I couldn't be leaving the job after us losing to Thomastown as well, even if it was altogether more competitive. We're definitely in the top three or four and pushing to reach the county final, but in my mind, 100 percent, my fourth year in 2023 is going to be my last as Carrickshock manager.

I was determined to make the most of it, never thinking we would be fighting relegation once again after a cruel run of injuries. But that's sport.

It always surprises. There are never any promises.

It what makes us love it too, I suppose.

There'll be other jobs beyond Carrickshock. I've no doubt about that.

I'll be spreading the net not too far down the line. There have been offers from inter-county teams and senior clubs in Waterford and Wexford and, living in Kilkenny, you're pretty much surrounded by a huge range of quality set-ups and it's definitely something I've got huge interest in.

I'll never, ever manage in the same grade against Carrickshock.

There were a few calls from other intermediate clubs when I hadn't committed to another year with the club, but I couldn't manage a team playing in the same grade.

That will never happen.

JAMIE

RICHIE CAME INTO the Carrickshock job when it wasn't as appealing as, say, 15 years previously when we were competing or at the very least, in contention for the senior title. I think he has steadied the ship and got us competitive again. The thing a lot of us aim to do after we stop playing is to give something back to the club; it was something dad was always big on, and that remains the case, so Richie deserves a lot of credit for taking the job on when he did because it was a very important time for the club. Carrickshock has always been to the fore with him. He's a very good coach.

JOHN

HURLING UNDER RICHIE as Carrickshock manager has been the finest. We don't talk too much about hurling away from matches and training, and that's working well for us; he knows he has a job to do as well. He took on the job at a stage after we'd gone down again to junior, John Tennyson was finishing up, John Dalton was considering going, we didn't know what Ricey's plans were and Jamie was starting to push on… so we were starting to lose leaders. But he introduced a few under-21 players and made us really competitive again, and we've improved every year that he's been manager. He's been consistently freshening things up, doing new training drills and he's kept things really interesting. He and the lads with him have a lot of good ideas and we've enjoyed the way he's gone about the job. And it's going to be interesting to see if he'll be managing or coaching when the next job comes along because he's very good at both. It's a massive commitment one way or the other.

NICKY BRENNAN

RICHIE JNR HAS done phenomenal work with the club in the last few years. I think he certainly has something to offer Kilkenny and while there's no expectation that

Derek Lyng and his team are going anywhere else fast, at the same time, if the Kilkenny County Board were smart, the leadership and wherewithal Richie has could be put to great use with our minors and under-20s. And if Kilkenny don't offer something to him, there are plenty of other counties who would give their eye teeth for someone like Richie.

★★★

RICHIE SNR

I REMEMBER IN 1991, the Monday before we played Tipp in the All-Ireland final, the crowd that was in Nowlan Park that night was phenomenal. They were on the sideline. We weren't going to be doing a lot six days away from a final, but the buzz that night was amazing – you knew that you were part of something special.

And nights like that, by and large, are being taken away from the game and I just hope it's not going to do damage looking down the line.

I'm of retiring age myself now and when Richie was on the panel, I used to love going in on a Wednesday night after working in Carlow… and sit in and enjoy the training. There used to be elderly people there, and they would have given their lives to their clubs – be it Piltown, Glenmore, the Village and so on – the kick they used to get going in there, but that's all gone now and that worries me. When a training session was over, there was nothing stopping those lads in the stand from going out onto the field and just saying hello to a player.

I don't think it was doing any harm.

But the night responsible for changing all this was in the run-up to the 2010 final against Tipperary, with Kilkenny chasing five in-a-row. The rumour got out that John Tennyson and Henry Shefflin had been down to Ger Hartmann in Limerick for treatment and that they were going to be back training, and naturally there was a huge interest in that session. But the plug was pulled on Nowlan Park being open the way it used to be after that, and I found that very disappointing.

Another thing that disappoints me is the way teams are named now.

When I played, your team was often named on the Tuesday of game week and if it wasn't named on the Tuesday, it was definitely named by Thursday. But we're in a situation now where you could have people working all week and they might go into their local on a Friday night, and they're looking forward to the game and the team still isn't named. – at least the team we all know will be starting. Naming a 'dummy team' is ridiculous and shows no respect to supporters. It's doing further damage to the relationship between management, players and supporters, and I really don't feel it's doing the profile of the game any favours.

And the profile of many of our leading hurlers isn't nearly as high as it ought to be. At the very least, hurlers shouldn't be wearing their helmets during the pre-match parades, so that the average supporter gets a proper chance to see their county players, along with the opposition. Take David Clifford in football... he is one of the most recognised sportspeople in the country already; he's like the Pied Piper signing jerseys after league matches because people recognise him, appreciate him and are drawn to him.

I think there's a case to be made for putting the names on the back of hurlers' jerseys and giving them the same number for the whole year because even this current Limerick team, all-conquering and brilliant as they are... outside of Limerick, how many would recognise most of those lads without a helmet or a familiar number on their jersey?

I've experienced that with Kilkenny over the past few leagues, wondering who certain players were because the minute they come out the helmets are on. We're not getting a chance to recognise them due to the faceguards. Ger Henderson, Joachim Kelly, Conor Hayes and others... they all wore helmets in my day, but everyone knew who they were. Of course, we need the helmets but there's still periods or parts of match day when they don't need to be on.

Bibs and tracksuits could have names on them as well – we have to build up the profiles of our players in a better way than we have up to now. Of course, not being recognised when things don't go well can be a help, but I think the friendship, the strength of the bond between players and supporters, could be irrevocably damaged.

A lot of supporters now go to matches, watch it and then that's it until the next game – there's no more talk about lads going well in training, which used to be part and parcel of the build-up to a match.

Genuine supporters loved that, and now it's gone completely.

I WAS NEVER singled out by a manager in a dressing-room when things weren't going too well for me. Now, Pat Henderson was hard in the dressing-room, but there was never anyone pointing a finger at someone and saying, 'You have five minutes to do something and if you don't… you're off'.

There was never anything like that.

I remember a period with my club in around 1991 and I was going through a bad phase. Shocking bad. I was so down on myself and so empty.

I knew I was, but I didn't need anyone to point it out to me. I was asking myself what I was at and what was going wrong, but there's not a player who doesn't go through that at some stage in their career.

But this is where I'd draw a big distinction between myself and Richie.

He has a different way of processing a poor performance. He's able to toss it out a window quickly, forget about it and move on to the next day. I was too hard on myself at times and that didn't help things at all. If I was over a team now and I saw a guy going through that, I'd sit down with him and say:

'Listen, this is going to turn. You're just going through a bad period. So, stick with it and things will come good again. The confidence will come back. I know there's more in you. More importantly, you know there's more in you. Trust what I'm saying. But trust yourself. You'll come good again.'

Both Richie and myself love golf and the way golfers have to train themselves mentally in order to remain successful is a lesson we could probably all tap into, be it in sport or life in general. You might hit a bad shot, but then you've got to move on and deal with the next shot and concentrate on making that as good a shot as you can. You might scramble to make the par, but you've made that par by concentrating on making the best of things on that particular hole. It's all about moving on, and that's something Richie has always been good at.

Richie has given the past four years to Carrickshock and management came a little bit sooner than he'd have anticipated given his knee injury. I always felt that he'd eventually go down that road at some stage, and I'm naturally thrilled that he has given those four years back to the club. Maybe he felt he didn't do himself justice in the two senior finals he played in… and we're talking about a time when the gambling was probably at its height.

I'm very proud of him taking on the job and sticking with it, because I know he has been approached numerous times by bigger club within that period. Sure, you'd have to admire that.

The other thing is that he took on the job when we were losing the likes of

John Dalton, John Tennyson and, of course, Richie himself – Michael Rice is still lining out, which says a hell of a lot about him as well.

He has done his bit for the club for now and who knows what lies down the line. We've got some good youngsters who'll feed their way into the team in three to four years' time, so I'd be optimistic about the future.

VII

The Power Legacy

★★★

★★★

ANN

THE ENTHUSIASM FOR hurling has never dipped in the slightest under our roof. Not with any of us. And we've Ruairí coming now, which is great; there's a continuity to it. Jamie and John are hurling away for the club and they still get a lot out of it. But sure, so do Richie and myself, and it's a great way to be.

I'd wouldn't swap it for anything.

In terms of inter-county hurling, bar two years, I think, given Richie's later involvement as a selector, we had someone in the house involved with Kilkenny… since Richie started as a minor back in '75 all the way through to Richie and John with the seniors in 2015. And all the success they all had made it all the more enjoyable for the whole family. It really was an amazing run, to end up with 13 senior All-Ireland medals won between the three of them.

One All-Ireland medal is special, so to have that many of them is just the stuff you'd dream about. It's a fantastic record.

★★★

RICHIE SNR

I ALWAYS FELT that I gave it my best.

Look, I know I had bad days in the county jersey, but I always felt that I prepared as well as I could prepare and I always gave it 100 percent. I was probably lucky enough given that I had a good All-Ireland final in 1982, I got the goal in '83 which was a huge turning point in that game… and to be part of a 'double

double' winning Kilkenny team has always been a source of huge pride to me.

We had 10-to-12 great years with that group of players.

You had to be as honest as you could to stay alive within that group because every one of them were brilliant individuals.

As for Richie, I think it was only when his career finished prematurely that maybe a lot of his fellow players realised what he had contributed to that unbelievable Kilkenny team, given his ability to create chances and take balls out of the sky. He produced some phenomenal performances, and it was quite something to be there in Croke Park so many times, watching a son of yours doing that in front of 80,000 people.

And to have both himself and John scoring goals in the same All-Ireland final was just beyond my wildest dreams. And then to have Jamie, Richie and John all playing and winning an All-Ireland intermediate title with the club was so incredibly special.

Talk about a proud day for Anne, myself, Stephanie and Suzanne.

I don't like talking about regrets, and I know I'm not the first person to have said this, but it's such a pity there wasn't a television camera to capture what was probably Richie's best ever performance... on a Sunday morning in Callan against James Stephens in a senior championship quarter-final in 2010 when we won by 1-20 to 1-15 – and I was a selector the same day.

I never, ever saw a player on fire like Richie was for 60 minutes that day. The Village had Jackie Tyrell, Peter Barry and Donnacha Cody playing, great backs the three of them, and Richie just ignited scoring 13 points... seven of them from play.

It will always stand out in my memory. It was an unreal performance. John Knox said as much in his *Kilkenny People* match report:

'And the one who slew the city dragon was the gifted Richie Power. Playing as the target man and 'running off the square' at full-forward he made himself available for every delivery and he had the silky touch to transform possession into account. Power rose the white (flag) an awesome 13 times, on eight occasions during the first-half, as he put hardship on the Stephens defence, and a number of players put against him. This was Power as we have never seen him before at club level; easing on to the ball, finding space where none appeared to exist, neatly combining with all around him and finishing with deadly accuracy often in the tightest of situations.'

Many people said it to me afterwards, that they'd never forget the way he hurled that day in Callan. I'm not blowing his trumpet; he's never needed that or sought it from anyone, but there were people standing outside our dressing-room afterwards and they were gob-smacked... they were in awe of what they were after seeing.

I remember a man, who was standing to the back of where the selectors and the manager were that day, and he said, 'We're seeing something today that we'll never see again'.

And he was right. It was 12 out of 10 stuff.

I never saw anything like it before or since.

Richie had some unbelievable games with Kilkenny and you'd be hoping that, as time goes on, that people will look back on what we've contributed over long years... 13 senior All-Ireland medals, eight for Richie, my own three, and John's two – and all three of us after scoring goals in All-Ireland finals. It's another lovely distinction and there's not many who've been under the same roof can lay claim to a record like that. It's not something we've ever spent too much, or any time, talking about that but you'd have to be proud of it too. To be honest, I'd never thought about it until it was pointed out to me during the preparation of this book. To score in All-Ireland finals and to win them was something.

We really were part of something special.

When it's happening in real time, you're living in a bubble. Yes, there were the kids, yes there was the house and, of course, there was Ann... but when you're in that hurling bubble, you're just consumed by it. And I'm as much in love with the game now as I was at my peak in a Kilkenny jersey.

But I do have a little bit of a concern about my own county: we're a small county compared to the Corks, the Tipps and Galways of this world. We have only 12 senior teams and 12 intermediate teams, and I do wonder if the day of getting three or four lads out of one house and all the way into a senior inter-county panel is history.

Maybe Kerry or Dublin might manage it, but I think those days are gone. But it could seriously impact the smaller counties. Will Offaly ever again have an era where three men from the same family – such as the Dooleys – will have such an impact? We've had the Hendersons – Pat, John and Ger, the Brennans from Conahy, the Fennellys from the Shamrocks and the Ryans from Clara, who have served Kilkenny so well in the past.

Times move on and families are smaller now, so there's certainly less of a chance of that happening down the line.

A lot of what's been recalled here might never have happened, though, and I still get a shudder when I think about getting into the Barry's Tea van one morning out in the yard after I'd finished loading it up. I used to have to take quite a sharp left coming out of our place at the time, the sort of thing we all do automatically most mornings.

Richie was only three or three and a half at the time, and he'd been out with me a good bit that morning, but as I was getting ready to head off, I assumed he'd gone back into the house. There wasn't sight nor sound of him.

I'd loaded the van, closed the back door and gently put my foot on the accelerator when I saw a small set of fingertips at the front of the van. Richie was stood there, looking at the headlights… when his hands came into view and I spotted him, after I'd only barely moved forward in the van.

For the three weeks after that, I wasn't right; I was restless thinking about what could have happened. For a long time after that, I couldn't get that morning out of my head. I just don't know what way I'd have been after that, only for spotting Richie's fingertips. Richie is in a brilliant spot now. He handled his off-field issue seriously well… and he knows himself now.

I'm delighted with what he's done with the club after putting four important years back into it. I know that he was head-hunted to go elsewhere but at least he knows he can walk out at the end of his fourth year as manager with his head held high. He's in a happy position and he has two sons now; he's where I was now when we had small children and that's a great place to be.

My own enthusiasm for hurling has never dropped an iota. Ann is as mad into it as I am, and we've never lost the drive for it. Between myself being involved with Kilkenny for so long and then the lads being involved after me, it was all-go when it came to hurling – and we've loved it all.

Then Ann drove the lads to training and matches for the club as often as I did. I don't think we'd change anything. Did I lose out on extra work opportunities and a bit more money on account of the hurling? Probably, but no money would have given us what we as a family, together, or what we got out of hurling between the club and the county.

I'd like to think we'd be remembered for having made a contribution to the development of the Carrickshock club and the success Kilkenny enjoyed across five different decades across all the grades. That'll be for other people to decide upon years from now - but I know that we always gave our very best.

★★★

NICKY BRENNAN

THE POWERS HAVE always worn their success very lightly. There's a trait in both Richie and Ann that never let any of the lads, be it in sport or in life, get above their station. They were always expected to work hard, just like their parents, and that sowed the seed for where they've all got to in their own lives. The fact that both Richies and John all scored goals in All-Ireland finals is a great distinction as well. As a family, they've a huge amount to be proud of.

★★★

RICHIE JNR

DAD WILL BE remembered as someone who literally worked his socks off and left absolutely everything that he had on the field from a hurling point of view, and from a Kilkenny point of view.

Most years, he would have started back training on St Stephen's Day by running around the farmers' field up the road, past the school in Stoneyford. Dad has often said to us that he was never the most skilful hurler and he felt that he had to get his fitness levels to a certain place that would surpass the more skilful players, who mightn't have been as fit as him... and he definitely did that.

When I was growing up, I used to love sitting down watching the 1982 and '83 All-Irelands; of course, Kilkenny lost the 1987 and '91 finals, but dad played in all four and he'd have featured in the '92 final only for an injury, one of the few he had as an inter-county player.

My first real All-Ireland memory of dad was the 1991 All-Ireland final against Tipperary – I was five going on six. Dad retired from inter-county the following year, so we never had the chance of being involved on a pitch invasion on All-

Ireland final day. Now he hurled on for years and years with the club, and I've no shortage of memories from that time; himself and Jamie hurled together in dad's last year with Carrickshock... so it's lovely to have that.

Dad was a clubman first and foremost, and that was instilled in all of us. Going to the club games and watching him for many years after that was very enjoyable and his attitude to the game never changed through those final years.

Enda McEvoy summed up dad as well as anyone ever did in a *Sunday Independent* interview before the 1990 championship.

'For the past eight years he's been paying his contribution fees – sometimes at centre-forward, sometimes on the wing, once or twice in the number 14 shirt, but mostly at midfield. Foraging, beavering, toiling to provide the link between defence and attack. Never stopping. And, as an intermediate club man, never having his 'own' selector to champion his cause. It's that work rate Richie Power is famous for in Kilkenny hurling circles. Having artists of the ash plant is all very well, but every team needs its unsung heroes to assemble the canvas for the masters to work on.'

From a club perspective, dad was chairman of the club in 1986 when he was still hurling and he won an All Star that year too. That just typifies him. He was a top player and a club administrator at the same time. Imagine anyone doing that nowadays?

There were Cork clubs knocking on his door when himself and mam were living down there but never in a million years would he have hurled for any of them. And I know for a fact is, if he was back there again, no matter what was on the table, he wouldn't have left Carrickshock. Just look at the years of service he's after giving since he stopped playing.

He managed me the whole way up from under-14 to intermediate and senior; we won two under-16 'A' county finals and two minor 'A' county finals under him, a huge achievement for a small, rural club. He was involved at under-21 and senior level as manager and selector, and he's been involved with our minors this year.

In my eyes, anytime you talk about Carrickshock, I think dad's name would be the first name that comes to the minds of people not from the parish. And then you have the likes of Pat Dwyer then as well, who was been a staunch Carrickshock man. I'm sure he has never thought about how he'll be remembered but I've no doubt he will be, and well beyond the parish as well; he has made friends all over the country through the GAA.

As for me?

Growing up, it was always my dream to put on a Kilkenny jersey. Mam has often said that I was quite an arrogant, cocky little fella when I was younger and I would have always, you know, maybe said that I was going to go on and play for Kilkenny. But I suppose, I realised that side of it at under-14, 16 and minor level and, obviously, to captain a minor team to an All-Ireland was huge for me.

And to go onto the senior team and enjoy such a level of success was something I'll always be very proud of. But the big thing for me was the hope that I'd have left the jersey in a better place than where it was when I took it on, and that would have been my only wish. Regardless of the success and the medals, and the personal accolades and all of that, for me that's what it's all about. It's about leaving the jersey in a better place for the next young chap to come in and take it on. And that's how I'd like to be remembered from a Kilkenny point of view.

In terms of the club, Carrickshock was, is and always will be everything to me. Club always came before county – 100 percent, 365 days a year. Carrickshock would always come first for me. Obviously, I suppose with our involvement with Kilkenny, it took us away from the training field and away from the club for long stints of the year. The harsh reality of it is that when I finished with Kilkenny, I more or less had to finish playing with Carrickshock.

When most players retire from inter-county, they go back to their clubs and hurl for five, six, seven years, and really enjoy club hurling and give back what the club have given to you growing up. But I didn't have that.

I tried my best for two years given the way my knee was and, luckily enough, we won an intermediate club All-Ireland title and got back up to the senior grade. But it was two years being a very bit-part player, I was only really involved to a certain extent. The future excites me.

Life beyond hurling excites me. Maria and I have been together for the past three years and we've a busy house with Ruairí, Cooper – Maria's son (the two boys started primary school together) – along with our youngest boy, who may well want to add a few chapters to this book looking down the line.

After all, with a name like Richie Óg, sure you couldn't rule anything out! And, yes, of course he'll be hurling for Carrickshock.

Now there's something to look forward to…

A SON FOLLOWING IN HIS FATHER'S FOOTSTEPS, AND NEVER STOPPING!

Richie Jnr celebrates the proudest day of his hurling career, when he overcame the injuries that ended his county career and helped Carrickshock to the All-Ireland Intermediate Club Championship in Croke Park in February 2017.

Richie on his Confirmation Day with his granny, Statia, and also in 2003 when he brought the All-Ireland Minor Championship trophy home after captaining Kilkenny. Out in force (below) at a Carrickshock fundraiser (from left) Stephanie and Doireann, mam, and me and Richie Óg.

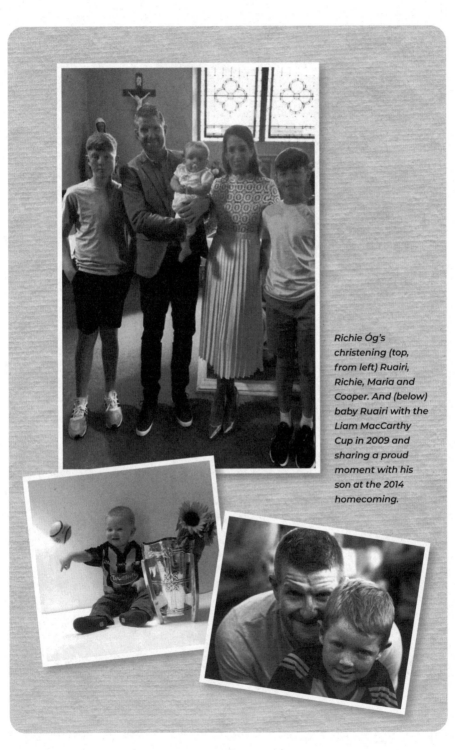

Richie Óg's christening (top, from left) Ruairi, Richie, Maria and Cooper. And (below) baby Ruairi with the Liam MacCarthy Cup in 2009 and sharing a proud moment with his son at the 2014 homecoming.

Brian Cody and Richie Jnr, with the Liam MacCarthy Cup and Irish Press Cup, after Kilkenny claimed the double in 2003 and (right) celebrating with Henry Shefflin three years later after the first of a four in-a-row was claimed with victory over Cork.

The Kilkenny team before clinching the 'Famous Four' by defeating Tipperary in 2009. And (right) Richie celebrates with the Liam MacCarthy Cup, and (below) Richie floats through with the ball during the game.

John and Richie Jnr and Snr the week before Kilkenny set out on an historic 'Five' All-Irelands in 2010 (John was lining out in the minor final), and (right) Richie takes in the defeat by Tipperary.

Richie followed in his father's footsteps with All Star awards! Here he is in 2011 after being voted the best in the land in his position, and (below) with his teammates on a triumphant night (from left, front row) Paul Murphy, Tommy Walsh and Richie Hogan, and (back row) Michael Rice, Henry Shefflin, Michael Fennelly, Brian Hogan and Richie Jnr.

Richie celebrates scoring on the double against Tipperary in the 2014 All-Ireland final and (right) he has company on the steps of the Hogan Stand, as he and Ruairi lift the Liam MacCarthy Cup.

Richie enjoys the perfect moment after winning the All-Ireland title in 2015, by having a 'father and son' timeout on the pitch, and the puckaround of a lifetime, with Ruairi.

The Carrickshock squad before the All-Ireland Intermediate Club Championship final victory over Ahascragh-Foghenach in Croke Park in February 2017.

Jamie Power celebrates with his Carrickshock teammates on a lap of Croke Park after winning the All-Ireland Intermediate title in 2017. and (right) captain John Tennyson lifts the trophy high. The Power family (below) enjoy their greatest day on the field (from left) Jamie, Richie Snr, Ruairi, Ann, John and Richie Jnr.

Richie and Maria, and Richie Óg, on a
family holiday in June 2023.

EPILOGUE

★★★

ANN

RICHIE AND MYSELF are from the same parish and would have known each other growing up, and we started going out around the time he hurled in the under-21 All-Ireland in 1977… when he scored a goal in the final against Cork in Thurles (we won by 2-9 to 1-9). We were a 'steady item' by the time Carrickshock won the county junior title in 1979, moved to Cork in January 1980, and we got married the following year.

James and Ellen Duggan were my parents and they had six of us – Margaret, Mary, Helen and Bridget… and I'm a twin to the one boy they had, Pat. I've loved gaelic games for as long as I can remember, and played camogie for Carrickshock until I was 44. The whole lot of us played it the whole way up… I was around 10, maybe 12 the first time I played a competitive match.

By then, Richie was over-40 as well and still playing, and he was onto me to retire… so I told him I'd retire when he retired. I brought the five children with me all the time I played. Sure, it was my outlet and I loved it.

When it came to going training, I had a great friend, Maura Roche, the Lord have mercy on her and she used to look after them – so they weren't really aware of me being out on the field, playing camogie. Then one day, Richard copped me at half-time, in terms of me not minding him more than anything, and he bawled for the whole of the second-half.

Richie was gone training the same nights I was training, when I'd have the five children with me, so it was never a case of me being a 'hurling widow' or anything like that. It's very hard nowadays to be hurling or playing camogie while being married and having small children – now it's not impossible – and the married players are very much in the minority given the demands of life, as much as the demands of the game.

Daddy was where I got my main love of camogie from; he was heavily involved with the camogie club and he was probably one of the first people in the village to have a car… and he used to load up the car – an Austin Cambridge – and bring us to the matches. When we started off playing with Carrickshock, we were all within a half mile of each other… you had three or four Daltons, two Walshs, two Aylwards, us five Duggans… along with the Tennysons and Barrons, all living within a small area.

Then a few other girls from a little further away got involved and that's how it all started. I'd be out most evenings after school, hitting the ball against the wall – that was the norm. We used to play mixed matches between the boys and the girls when we were small and those matches wouldn't take you too long to toughen up. It used to be great fun. I loved it.

I always played in the forwards, so between Richie and myself, it's no surprise that Richard and John followed suit at that end of the field; but then Jamie was an excellent goalkeeper, so we ended up covering both ends well!

We were playing Glenmore one day and my youngest sister, Bridget was on the line for Glenmore that day. She married Paddy Murphy, so their children, Eoin, the current Kilkenny goalkeeper (I stood for him at his Confirmation) and his brother, Alan are my nephews. Anyway, that day in Glenmore, my daughter, Stephanie was in goal for us and, for some reason I still don't understand, I started at centre-back.

When you're used to playing in the forwards, the natural thing is to ramble closer to the goal, which is exactly what I did. Well, more than once the cry came up from my daughter, the goalkeeper… 'Mammy, will you effing come back and mark up?'

And then I'd reply, 'Will you call me Ann!'

Of course, the sister was having a right skit on the line with all this. Stephanie and myself played a couple of years together and we got on fine.

Back in the early summer (of 2023), at the launch of the AstroTurf pitch in Hugginstown, we had a past players match – a mixed match – so I came on at half-time, and Stephanie and young Richie were both on the other team. And even with the bad knee, when he came on, he nearly turned the whole match around.

That was great craic – and I was the oldest one togged out... the first time in 22 years since I last played. Everyone on the line had a good laugh as well. The two lads weren't too near to me during the match, which probably worked out best for all concerned! But it was a lovely night. Sure, if you could play forever, who wouldn't?

HURLING WAS THE only outlet we had.

When we'd go to a wedding, while Richie was hurling for the county, as soon as the meal was over, you went off home, even for the league days. I'd remember people sneering at us, saying, 'What are you doing going home, sure it's only a league match'.

But that's what Richie felt he had to do, and I was 100 percent behind him on that. Every match was serious to him and meant something to him. He had great discipline when it came to Kilkenny, and it stood to him. But the two of us were of one mind when it came to stuff like that... sure, we were in Páirc Uí Chaoimh two days after having Jamie, for a big Cork senior championship match. Now that might sound mad to some people, but that's how things have worked in this house, and we've found a way to make it work well.

Both Richie and myself loved Cork.

We still do. Life had been good to us down there, putting our sadness to one side, but then the opportunity to come back home arose with the Barry's Tea job offer. Had that not come up when it did, I wouldn't have minded staying in Cork at all. If we'd stayed, Richie Jnr would have been born in Cork. Imagine the craic we'd have had with a divided house, the older brother a Kilkenny man and his two younger brothers in the red of Cork?

God, we'd have got some mileage out of that!

But it was hardly the biggest inconvenience in the world to come back to the parish either. We were surrounded by our families and so many people we'd both grown up with and sure things could hardly have gone much better.

The 1982 All-Ireland final was special.

The following year, Kevin Hennessy took the paint off the post and had it gone in, we'd have been beaten by a point – but wide it went, and we won by two points (2-14 to 2-12). I was sitting beside Michael Madden, from Barry's Tea and he turned around to say something to me… but I was gone off through the wire and out onto the field to celebrate!

FOR ALL HIS success, I think Richie Junior was probably capable of being better than he was, if he had to fully apply himself. By his own admission he wasn't the greatest trainer in the world. Look, he liked to party – but not all the time.

None of the lads of Richie's age could get away with much when it came to the Kilkenny set-up. They couldn't do anything without it being reported back, and being brought to the floor. Himself, Cha and John Tennyson went to Waterford, ended up at a party in Kilmacow, but word got back. They went into training the next night. Richie had put in a really good session but the management said they wanted a chat with the three of them – and the three of them immediately knew what they were going to be asked about. Richie rang me on his way back to St Pat's and he told me, 'I came within a hair's breadth of being dropped off the panel, and only for there was more than one us… and Cha being captain, I wouldn't have been surprised if I'd been out the door'.

When he finished playing minor, Richie got a lovely letter from Brother Damien Brennan, the Lord of Mercy on him, thanking him, and telling Richie that he (Br Damien) had needed Richie a lot more than Richie had ever needed him.

Br Damien had a great influence on so many young players and loads of them went to visit him, including Michael Fennelly. That letter to Richie was a lovely gesture. Br Damien died in 2019. He was only 59. He was such a tremendous influence on Richie and so many other hurlers.

However much I love hurling, it's hard to see where much of the enjoyment is now in being an inter-county hurler. Sure, they have no life outside of it. To me, it was one of the reasons John pulled out, he just wasn't enjoying it.

In 2015, it was lovely to see both Richard and John playing in the Kilkenny team on All-Ireland final day, and both of them scoring goals. Will that ever happen again, to have two lads coming from such a small club, both making it into such a competitive team and then both scoring goals on the biggest day of the hurling year?

It's an amazing thing to have happened.

There are no guarantees in life and we've no All-Ireland won since 2015. We were spoiled by what that Kilkenny team achieved but no success lasts forever. It'll be the same with the current Limerick team at some stage, no doubt. But God, it was some run we had all the same.

Great times.

Richie played in an All-Ireland minor semi-final, two minor All-Ireland finals, three under-21 finals – including an under-21 and a senior final in the same year – and ended up playing in all the following All-Ireland senior finals Kilkenny reached up to 2015, winning eight Celtic Crosses. He has a lot to be proud of.

Carrickshock had a good crop of players when Richie was developing. I remember when Richie (Snr) was training them at under-12; after he'd had them for a few sessions he came home one night and told me there were four lads in the panel who would play senior hurling:

'Dalton, Tennyson, Rice… and our own lad."

He had them picked out even then. And he was right.

There are 13 senior All-Ireland medals under this roof, along with the underage All-Irelands and the All-Ireland win with the club – and John won a soccer All-Ireland with Kieran's too. There's been great success but we don't have the medals all out on display here. I suppose we've never been too inclined to talk about our own. And I've often met genuine people who say to me, 'Sure why not talk all the successes up? You're entitled to'.

But we've never done that.

No one in Kilkenny ever really has, I think. But don't get me wrong: there's nothing like winning an All-Ireland and all that follows it. It's an unbelievable feeling.

Richie Jnr could see someone else out of the corner of his eye and give him the ball, while some lads mightn't. When Tipperary's Padraic Maher retired from inter-county hurling in 2021, he was asked who was the most difficult player he'd marked and, while he mentioned Henry Shefflin and Joe Canning, he said Richie was the most difficult of all.

In an article which a nice man from Thurles sent us, Padraic said you'd have to be up early, wide awake and have your wits about you any day you were marking Richie. It was a great compliment.

Not winning a senior championship with the club will always be the big regret as far as Richie is concerned. Carrickshock got to those two finals and they really should have won at least one of them. That, in his mind, would have completed the set. But to get back to Croke Park for the All-Ireland club final, and to have the three lads on the team that day, that was incredibly special. That was a huge day for us all.

There's nothing like hurling.

Nothing comes close to it. I remember when Richie (Snr) was playing, there was no guarantee that he'd be starting a match for Kilkenny – you didn't know until pretty much the last minute. That's a lot different now, of course. And I remember when John was in training, I'd be asking him every night about training – sure, I must have been driving him mad… asking him if he was on the 'A' or the 'B' team?

And he'd tell me he was on the 'B' team, but sure that was the place to be… and he worked himself into the starting team in 2014. He hurled well and earned his place.

There's been so many high points over the years but Richie scoring the winning point in the 2003 All-Ireland minor final was extra special. And he scored some very important goals when the seniors needed one of course.

To be out on the field with Ruairí after the 2015 final was great for the two of them, and there was probably at least another three years in him after that, if the knee had stayed right. He was starting to get really focused about his preparation by then.

The years only flew by.

★★★

JAMIE

WHEN MAM AND dad were living in Cork – both Stephanie and myself were born down there – dad was still coming back up the road to hurl with Kilkenny and Carrickshock. The easier choice would have been for him hurl for a club in Cork but he never saw that as a viable option. Hurling, Carrickshock and Kilkenny… it's all we've ever known.

Everything was built around matches… holidays, summers, the whole lot.

Beating the ball off the gable end every evening after school, that was our regular every day thing to be doing… and we just loved it.

Dad often talked about buying pubs and he'd have looked at a few pubs down through the years in other parishes elsewhere in Kilkenny. Sure, there'd have been murder if we'd been moving to the likes of Tullaroan, if that had happened at a time when we were old enough to be playing. That would have been way harder than if we'd stayed in Cork. Daddy just bleeds Carrickshock and his commitment to the club has always been massive. And he still takes everything to do with the club to heart.

When we were relegated in 2015, I came in the back door at Christmas Week and mam said, 'Will you go in and talk to him?'

He wasn't going to the pub after the relegation; it was like there'd been a death in the family. Sure, I went into the sitting-room and told him to cop on. It shows how much the club means to him.

He is a perfectionist. He's always been inclined to be busy. But I'd like to think that all five of us have a very strong work ethic. We all work hard and when we do something, we try to do it right. We've always applied ourselves to whatever we've been asked to do and we're not afraid to work. And that ethic comes from mam and dad.

BEING OLDER THAN the rest of the lads, I'd have a few memories of dad playing. In the '91 All-Ireland final, when I'd have been 11, he was marking John Leahy and he'd a really good first-half – the two of them used to meet each other out on the road so that was an interesting match-up. Then in '92 dad came back and was brought on as a sub in the Leinster final against Wexford.

I got to hurl one year with Dad… in 1997. I was 16 and started at corner-forward alongside him in a few league games. At that age, I was just delighted to be playing; I wasn't really thinking too much about dad being a few yards away from me for most of the match. But I look back now and I'm glad that happened.

Not too many sons get to hurl with their fathers nowadays.

Richie's juvenile group was a golden era for our club... Michael Rice, John Tennyson, John Dalton, and himself of course. They won under-14, under-16 and two minor 'A' titles, which was unprecedented in the history of our club... and dad did a good bit of work with them. But he always saw the best in everyone. He persisted with some lads, whether they were lacking a bit of skill or effort but that's probably what you have to do with a small club.

Sure, just look at his record as a manager. Wherever he went, the teams he managed were successful and, of course, he had the under-21 All-Ireland title in '99 with Kilkenny when I ended up in goal.

Now, I wasn't originally involved beyond the trials – dad felt a bit odd about it; he didn't want anyone accusing him of favouritism if he'd picked me. I'd been the county minor goalkeeper the previous year. I was getting ready to go out after playing a junior match over in Dunnamaggin when he told me he'd no 'keeper for a challenge match against Tipp in Thurles the following morning.

I'd say I gave the best display I ever had in goal that Sunday, making three outrageous saves and that's how I ended up in the team... and ended up with an All-Ireland medal. But dad set the standards on and off the field... and he still does.

Richie has, by any measure, an amazing record. But despite the eight All-Ireland medals, I don't think we ever saw him operating to the height of his potential. That alone goes to show how good a hurler he was, and we probably saw what he was capable of in 2014 after the good pre-season. Despite the cruciate injury against Galway, he got back in time to make an impact in the All-Ireland final and for both himself and John to score goals in the replay was something special. He was as skilful as he was headstrong. But there was still more in him.

I'd always have been pretty hard on Richie.

I'd have always worked hard when it came to hurling, but I've have always told him when he hurled well too. We did our best to be constructive to each other; we weren't having shouting matches in the kitchen about hurling.

If any of us had ever come in the door at home after winning a medal with any big ideas, that wouldn't have been long getting kicked to touch. That's always been the attitude in the family when it comes to success with the club and the county.

I think that's been a huge thing for us.

★★★

STEPHANIE

I'VE ALWAYS HAD a fondness for Cork.

Much of that is down to how warmly mam and dad have always spoken about it and their friends down there, Tom and Tess, who are like family to us – I also went back to Cork, where I'd a ready-made family. Dad could have ended up playing for a club there and if he had, sure there'd have been Cork jerseys in the washing machine rather than Kilkenny ones!

During his peak playing years, he was up every morning at 6am.

When we were young, we used to go out and help fill the van up with tea, and then head off with him. Both mam and dad worked very hard throughout that time. And while myself and Suzanne weren't playing at the top level, I still loved playing. I didn't love it as much as the lads, however, and I admire what they gave up to be as good as they've been.

And when I went away and worked in Australia, I never lost my love for it. I probably enjoyed watching the lads playing a lot more than I enjoyed playing camogie myself. To see them all on the field when Carrickshock won the county intermediate final, after so much heartache, was so special. Suzanne loves it too and she was a better player than I was.

Mam and dad have always been hard workers but they've never forgotten the social side of things and how important it is to enjoy themselves. They've been off on a few holidays and that's been lovely to see – they've worked hard all their lives to make trips away possible. We know how hard they had to work to provide for us. They couldn't head off like that when they were younger, but now they can… and they deserve it.

I'd say no-one in Kilkenny enjoyed the 2014 All-Ireland win as much as mam and dad. They got such a kick out of it, having the two lads playing and then both scoring goals – the village was buzzing. I'd had an operation the previous Tuesday so I was sat at home watching the match with two neighbours of mine, and I'll never forget it.

John had told me on the Friday night that he was starting the following day – he'd told no one else by then. I was absolutely delighted for him but I was devastated for myself since I knew I wouldn't be going.

'Well, the two of ye better both score goals,' I warned him.

And that's exactly what happened. And then I actually missed both the goals because I was out the back… it was so nerve-racking! I ended up going down to the local that night and it was an amazing night. We'd had great nights before that but that stood apart. Carrickshock was so proud of all the lads that made the step-up with Kilkenny.

The lads have always been incredibly supportive of each other, sat around the kitchen table, going through a game and it was always enjoyable to listen to them. Jamie would be that bit more direct, while dad would make us laugh with a skit during it all, but no one ever fell out because of a conversation about hurling.

Winning the Intermediate All-Ireland in 2017 and having all three lads involved was amazing. Richie was effectively playing on one good leg, while the bad knee was heavily strapped and the only full game he played that year was the final in Croke Park. I was going to Cork for a hen night, I think, and I'd put on the radio to hear how they were doing when they played Celbridge in the Leinster final.

Then I turned it off when they were seven points down… I was convinced the game was over. For some reason, I flicked back over to it on the car radio and I had to pull in to the side of the road to listen to the last three minutes of the match… when three late goals swung the game for us.

It was daylight robbery… but talk about exciting!

★★★

JOHN

YOU WOULDN'T BE going too far wrong in describing dad as the ultimate clubman. To be chairman of the club while he was working full-time for Barry's Tea, working Friday and Saturday nights in Hennessey's… and hurling for Kilkenny, and that was around the time the house was being built as well.

Just imagine any inter-county hurler doing all that now?

I know things were different back then in terms of training and all that, but at the same time, he was so committed to everything he did. Nothing was ever done by halves.

Dad would only say something to me about my own hurling if he felt it needed to be said. Most of the time, he'd leave it to yourself when we'd come in after a match, but if you were going bad, then he'd have a word. Even when we were involved with Kilkenny, mam would be the one talking hurling… morning, noon and night, whereas dad might talk to you for 10 minutes about it, then get a cup of tea and head off to the sitting-room.

It's nice to be part of a rare group of All-Ireland final goalscorers given that dad, Richie and myself have seen the green flag raised for Kilkenny on the big day in Croke Park. I've never spent too much time thinking about it, but when you think of the size of our club as well, sure you could only be proud to be part of something like that.

It was a huge year for both Richie and myself, in 2014.

It was probably the first time Richie had ever put in a proper pre-season between hard training and the gym work with Mickey Comerford. He'd been told the previous autumn that he wasn't going to be part of Kilkenny's plans – it was pure Cody psychology – and Richie trained like he never did before after that.

Even to this day, he goes up to the field before we train and he'll do 45 minutes in the gym. In his early career, he never did anything to that level. But even now, his first touch is exceptional… he turned out in a few junior matches in the past couple of years, with pretty much no training done – sure he can't on account of the knee – and his eye wasn't remotely out. That's natural talent for you.

He really should still be hurling now, let's face it.

As a family, we've had a great run of it, going back to dad in terms of big wins, but you'd have a job to find a few of our medals at home! Any time we'd go to a medal presentation, be it the club or the county, as soon as you'd be off the stage, it was handed to mam… and she'd put it in the bag, and that'd be it. I doubt if I've seen any of them since the presentation nights.

★★★

SUZANNE

MAM AND DAD are both very grounded people. When we were growing up, everything they did was for us. They were so good to us the whole way along –

and still are. The message, essentially, was that the five of us were just the same as everyone else, no better or no worse, whether we were good at gaelic games, school or anything else for that matter.

I think that's probably the reason that we've never made too much of the family's successes, proud and all as we are of all of them.

They're such a brilliant team... they've been hard workers their whole lives and the importance of hard, honest work was a message they made plain to us while we were kids. The devotion they've had to the club from the first time they were inside the gate of the field would be well known in the parish, and there was never really any stopping them... it was go, go, go all the time, between the five of us being brought here and there, and both mam and dad working full-time in between it all.

They just never stopped.

Dad was on the road the whole time, and then chairing the club... and winning an All Star at the same time was pretty unbelievable. I wasn't born when dad was hurling for Kilkenny so I'm reliant on stories that predate my arrival. But he would tell you without hesitation that he couldn't have done it without mam. She was minding kids while dad was going all the time, but that shows you how strong their connection was then... and still is now.

They found a way to make things work, and supported each other each every day. Between chats at home, and what neighbours would have mentioned over the years, I've a good grasp on how much he did for the club and the county, and for the lads in general before I was born. And, always, mam was there for him and us.

Richard was very unfortunate when it came to the injuries that ended up taking a good number of years off his career with Kilkenny. Just as he was approaching his prime, things took a turn for the worse which was obviously a huge setback. Mentally, it can't have been easy, especially when he was a hurler in the public eye both in Kilkenny and right across the country. There was always that pressure and expectation to perform well. And, of course, there was the natural expectation that he'd bring that inter-county form to club level, so when he didn't perform for Carrickshock the way he'd naturally expect of himself, that was a blow too.

Look, there's no escaping the fact that he clearly had great times – eight All-Irelands is a level of achievement not too many have to look back on – but the injuries definitely robbed him of something, both in terms of the county and the club.

Just like dad, Richard has always been very grounded about his hurling, despite the talk there'd have been about him since his teens. He never came across as arrogant or in any way cocky. Just look at him after the full-time whistle in all the All-Ireland finals he played in... the first hand he was looking to shake was his opponent. And he's always been good at making time for people after a match, on the side of a road or inside in Kilkenny on the street. He's always placed a lot of value in making time for others.

I'd have gone out with him after most of the All-Ireland wins and even when he was enjoying his drink, he'd still make time for people – even though he'd be a total messer with me at the same time. He always wore his success lightly, just as dad did before him.

★★★

JOHN KNOX

THE TWO RICHIES, Richie Senior's brothers – John, Maurice, Willie and Pat – and Richie Junior's brothers, Jamie and John. Not only did they play, but the Powers have been officials, they've been club officers, they've been driving forces behind club fundraisers and so on – while Richie Snr remains the big driver of the Carrickshock Golf Classic.

For Richie Jnr to win eight All-Irelands – it's an exceptional achievement, though I know how much he wanted Carrickshock to succeed, and he says he'd exchange all eight All-Ireland medals for one Kilkenny senior title. It shows how much the club wanted it.

It would have made an indelible mark on the history of the club, but the Powers' legacy in the lore of Carrickshock is already secured. It's a small club with limited playing resources, which has done remarkably well when you consider the competition in Kilkenny. But I do know the point he's trying to make. I understand the depth of the feeling that he's had given how close they got to that senior title.

That Richie Jnr played in the 2017 All-Ireland Intermediate final was incredible. He used to be on a warm-up bike for about a half an hour before matches to get the joint going. I have a problem with my knee, and it jars, and you can feel the bone on bone... but there he was running around Croke Park... which is a solid surface, far from your typical pitch.

He ran around during an All-Ireland final... with bone on bone in that injured knee. For all his honours, Richie Jnr is one of the most remarkable hurlers Kilkenny has ever had and I still get the feeling that the level of his talent is very underestimated. He was 15 when he came onto the Kilkenny minor team and he hurled at that grade for three years, captained them to an All-Ireland and then from there he was elevated straight into the senior team. He had come through St Kieran's as the star player as well; he had to handle all that, and you have to remember that everyone interested in Kilkenny hurling was talking about him. But he carried it all, which was something else for a lad of his age.

Yet when there was a lot of talk about those Kilkenny players who were on the brink of an eighth All-Ireland medal, be it Jackie Tyrrell, Eoin Larkin, Henry Shefflin of course and a good few more, it was almost overlooked going into the 2015 final that Richie was in line for his eighth too... and I'm not too sure why that was!

Something Monsignor Tommy Maher said about Mick Crotty springs to mind. 'Mick Crotty never had to go and prove himself any day,' he remarked, 'because no one ever outplayed him.' That sentiment would be equally true of Richie Power Jnr as well. I used to look at Richie at times during matches and I say to myself... *Richie, will you shift your ass?*

And then after years of watching him, I realised he had this languid style and that it worked so well for him. He was a long strider and he didn't seem to be pushing himself... but he always was! But that long stride of his gave him pace that was deceptive.

And he had this lovely weaving way with the ball on his hurley – Chunky O'Brien used to do it in a more flamboyant way – but Richie could chase the field with the ball on his stick.

What he achieved and how he hurled never got to his head. I'd say that's probably where the family background and club background told, and helped him to stay grounded. He was one of the best who grew up with a very bright flame in his career and the way he carried it was something else.

When Richie Power Jnr was picked for Kilkenny, all of the Powers were picked. Everyone came behind Richie and he had a massive family support system behind him, which was backed up by a great club support.

RICHIE SNR WAS the most giving player, in fact he was one of the most giving players Kilkenny ever had. I'd say he was a dream for Pat Henderson.

Once Richie was given the jersey, regardless of position or the role he was asked to perform, he gave every last breath that was in him for Kilkenny. In the 1982 All-Ireland final, he scored four points from play. He wore a black helmet that day and it almost came down a little bit on his eyes. He got lost in the flow of the game for a while and then, like that, in the second-half he put long range points together.

That was probably the game of Richie's life as an inter-county hurler, the sort of display every boy that picks up a hurley dreams of. That'll always be a special day for him.

The successes in 1982 and '83 were double doubles. To win the league and championship in both years, that was almost unheard of at the time because the thinking then was that if you put too much into the league, it'd hurt you come the championship. But Pat Henderson, in fairness just let them flow through. He was a great manager and a very intelligent man.

And while Pat had tactics, of course, he didn't tie his players into tight game plans; he was able to draw the best out of people. Henderson had a sense of discipline that those Kilkenny lads all bought into, and Richie was one of his most trusted players.

Give Richie a job to do, that's okay… that's that position looked after.

No manager ever had to worry about Richie. His head was always in the right space. He just had it. He was never afraid of any tackle. Even if Richie knew he was going to get hurt, he'd never hold back.

Brian Cody made it simple: the team that wins the All-Ireland in any year is the best team in the country. People may make other arguments… but the team that wins the MacCarthy Cup has the status. It was said by a few that the 1979 win was the worst Kilkenny team to win the All-Ireland. What a ridiculous thing to say!

They were the best team in Ireland that year. On any given year, to be All-

Ireland champions stands on its own. That was a great era for Kilkenny. The 'double double' was a massive achievement, and Richie was a huge part of that. That group of players remain great friends though Richie made friends all over the country… in Offaly, Galway and so on. And I mean great friends. And those friendships are pure. It's amazing. I don't know if players are as warm and friendly now with each other. I don't think they can be. But the bind between lads who hurled against each other 30 or 40 years ago remains so strong.

Richie remains so invested and enthusiastic about hurling.

He'd talk every day about it. So does Ann, who has been such a consistent support all through the years in whatever role Richie Snr played along with their five children. She knows her game and she'd put you in your place quicker than anyone. She played camogie and football into her forties.

They're beautiful people. I'm not just saying that because they're Kilkenny people… I'm saying that because I've known them for a long, long time. They're just good.

Richie Jnr, in a sense, drifted to greatness. And I don't mean in the sense that he didn't put in the effort. I mean in the sense that people didn't see the greatness that was unfolding in front of them. And again, like his father, he wasn't afraid to go into the tough places, and he was well able to look after himself.

I remember one day when somebody was a bit nasty with him, but he bided his time and when the opportunity arose, he sent a reminder to the lad marking him… listen, don't try that again.

I don't ever remember anybody pushing Richie Jnr aside or knocking him out of the game. Like his father, he never had to prove himself.

He was never cleaned out.

But then he kept hurling with the club until 2017. And again, it was done quietly. How many hours did he spend on his fitness, when he couldn't run the field with the lads? And how did he keep his touch in, and go on to play an All-Ireland final with his club?

That again goes back to what we were talking about; that, for me, as a player people didn't fully appreciate his genius. They probably didn't fully appreciate his commitment because, when the lads were running through the mud preparing for that All-Ireland, he was probably in the gym on the bike, keeping himself going… so it was remarkable that he was able to do to play an All-Ireland final.

He was still marking a good opponent, because the other team were champions in their own county, and they were champions of the province. So, he wasn't being marked by a bluffer, he was out against a good player and he still got the business done. He had the temperament, he had the experience of course to tap into as well, but still he had to drag a knee… a knee that wasn't cooperating, that wasn't prepared to twist and turn. He just had it.

As a manager and selector, Richie Snr would always have kept an eye on other sports and, unlike other GAA people, he had no fear in stepping outside the boundaries to do something a little different, like bringing in the sports psychologist for the Kilkenny under-21s in 1999. Other sports do it, so why not the GAA? I remember talking to one county manager and I asked him would he ever think about a psychologist?

'I'm the psychologist!' was the reply, whereas in Richie's case, if he felt he could get a further one percent out of the group, then he'd take whatever step required to find it.

That 1999 All-Ireland under-21 panel provided the backbone for what followed at senior level under Brian Cody. And that was a very important win, as it was achieved during what was, by Kilkenny standards, a low ebb off the back of two successive senior final defeats. We needed a serious injection of talent, which Ned Quinn acknowledged at the time, although nobody knew then that it would lead to such riches. But it did.

Richie brought in Eddie Brennan after seeing him hurl one night for his club. Richie took a chance on Eddie. He showed no fear in making that decision, just like bringing in Brendan Hackett, the sports psychologist. Everything was worth exploring. That under-21 panel was a gift to Kilkenny that a lot of people, even now, probably don't realise fully in hindsight. Most people will look back and say that Brian Cody won all those All-Irelands… but someone had to polish those players.

Richie went for the Kilkenny senior job which Cody got at the time. But he wore whatever disappointment he felt about that very lightly. He wears all these things lightly, because his idea has always been to try and make a contribution for the greater good. It was never for Richie Power's good.

I'd never say he has ever thought, *Oh, yes, that could have been me.*

That's just not the sort of people the Powers are. There's not a hint of that in any of them. What you see is what you get with the Powers. The cliché about doing exactly what it says on the tin… that's the Powers.

If you go to any of those places where Richie Snr has managed, where he has worked, where he has met people and made friends with them, you won't find anyone with a bad word to say about him. A gentleman is the word that always pops up.

A fierce competitor?

Absolutely, but always a gentleman.

He was up and down that road from Cork in a shagged car. An old Charade. On bad roads, as most roads in the 80s were. It wasn't exactly a Ferrari Richie was driving! And it must have been really hard going on the worst of nights during the winter. That alone was difficult. But he wanted to do it.

That's the mark of the man.

IN 2010, I'D HAVE been closer to the group of players and their line of thinking as opposed to listening to public sentiment about the 'Drive for Five'.

But I thought everything had been closed off among players and management when it came to the five in-a-row talk. With Richie Snr, we'd had the 'double double' and we'd had a few sniffs at a three in-a-row. But then we got three… and then we got four.

And the general public did get giddy, probably. But I didn't see anything that would have been worrying from the squad's perspective. It just didn't happen.

Closing off training at Nowlan Park?

I always felt that was sad. This silly idea was thrown about French students coming over and cackling on the sideline, bring noisy and so on. There were old men who would go across there every night, and meet and sit and munch, and be entertained. As Martin Fogarty said, sure how couldn't you be happy being involved with Kilkenny when you're watching the best players playing every night.

And people of a certain generation used to love going across and it's a pity that that had to be taken away from them – and now it's gone probably forever. Now, things like the 'Meet and Greet' with the players – where they meet their fans before All-Irelands – I understood why that was done away with, because it was an absolute drain on players and it became a distraction more than a help. Even though they were always conscious that you have to be fair to the fans.

But closing off training was a big loss.

It was a loss to a lot of people won't understand, but here it was a part of life, to ramble across to Nowlan Park and see what's going on. I'll give one example: I know a lad called Mick Dunne, who had worked for years in Dublin and then he came back to live in Kilkenny, and he used to go over to Nowlan Park and he'd tell me about training… who was going well and so on. He loved to see the training and make his own assessment, and he'd be at all the matches too. And that was just one person, so it's a pity what happened with training.

My first year with the *Kilkenny People* was in 1974, so I've seen most of our senior and underage victories over the years. I couldn't have asked for a more eventful and successful time to be reporting on inter-county hurling. What's been achieved given our population is extraordinary.

Our share of All-Ireland tickets is based on how many clubs we have, so we've always had a problem with getting tickets for finals, but still I always reckoned about 16,000 to 18,000 would cater for the people in Kilkenny who wanted to go an All-Ireland, you know, by and large… apart from the five in-a-row year when the demand was probably bigger.

But it is remarkable, taking our population size and our club numbers into account, that we did win so much. And there's not a word strong enough to explain what happened during the Cody era… to win 11 All-Irelands!

But the one thing that Kilkenny always had, and Mick Dempsey said it… there was always unity, there was no big bust-up in the dressing-room. The players would knock lumps off each other in club hurling, but we didn't have fractious championships, we had competitive championships. Take the Fenians for example, who had a ferocious rivalry with James Stephens in the 70s and 80s at a time when both clubs had five players each on the panel.

Mick Dempsey said that he couldn't understand when the Kilkenny lads came into training, just how much they left their club allegiances outside the dressing-room door.

COULD RICHIE JNR be a future Kilkenny senior manager?

Well, if he feels he has a strong enough apprenticeship served, why not? Like, he's been through it. At inter-county, he had just the one manager who achieved like no other. He has worked under different people at the club, so he has had a good education about the game.

The Powers are traditionalists in their hurling ways, but he has seen all the changes that have come about, and those things that can give you an edge… just like his father did, bringing in the psychologist and so on. Why not?

He could be the same as a manager. That same genius, that quiet genius that he had as a hurler could emerge. Because even the troubles in his private life could yet prove great strengths for him as a manager. He showed some character to get through that. He had the strength to go and seek help. He's an awful lot in his locker to bring to life, let alone to hurling.

Post-2015, who's to say that Richie wouldn't have made a difference here and there to get us one or two more All-Irelands? That's the thing, people don't realise … that this lad was 28 when he finished. Eight All-Irelands by 28 is phenomenal. When I was growing up the benchmark was John Doyle and Christy Ring… eight each. We ended up with one player with 10… and the rest, a bunch of them, with nine… and loads with eight.

Amazing stuff.

Kilkenny hurlers and fans just love success. They love winning. Cody always said if it's worth togging out for a match, it's worth trying to win it.

And that's a great, effective simplicity. That will to win has been there all the time. In all my years, only once would I say I saw a performance in a league match that I thought, maybe Kilkenny could have tried a bit harder. Once in 40 whatever number of years is not a bad record by any measure.

The people who have gone before us have left that gift to us, that there's no use being second. You have to be the best that you can be, and the fans love it. I don't think Kilkenny people see themselves spoiled with success.

They see it purely along the lines of… we won it, nobody handed it to us.

You can stand still and whinge, or you can be active and start leading… and that's what they do here in this county.

And in that respect, you'll find no one more committed than the Powers.

BIBLIOGRAPHY

★★★

Kilkenny GAA Yearbook, 1998 & 1999 (Kilkenny GAA County Board)

Larkin, Eoin: *Camouflage: My Story* (Reach, 2019)

Smith, Raymond: *The Hurling Immortals* (Bruce Spicer Ltd, 1969)

Townsend, Mark: *Brother Damien Brennan: The Silent Man Behind the Kilkenny Success Story* (Mark Townsend, 2023)

Wenger, Arsène: *My Life in Red and White* (Hachette UK, 2020)

Wooden, John (with Steve Jamison): *Wooden: A Lifetime of Observations and Reflections On and Off the Court* (McGraw Hill, 1997)

The Irish Examiner

The Irish Independent

The Sunday Independent

The Sunday Times

The Kilkenny People

The Meath Chronicle

GAA.ie

The GAA Social podcast (BBC Sounds)